The mind of the intelligent man will ponder a parable . . .

Sirach 3:29

Unearthing Your Ten Talents

Also available from
Sophia Institute Press®
by Kevin Vost:

Memorize the Faith!

Fit for Eternal Life

Kevin Vost, Psy.D.

Unearthing Your Ten Talents

A Thomistic Guide to Spiritual Growth
through the Virtues and the Gifts

SOPHIA INSTITUTE PRESS®
Manchester, New Hampshire

Sophia Institute Press
Box 5284, Manchester, NH 03108
1-800-888-9344
www.SophiaInstitute.com

Sophia Institute Press® is a registered trademark of Sophia Institute.

Library of Congress Cataloging-in-Publication Data

Vost, Kevin.
    Unearthing your ten talents : a Thomistic guide to spiritual growth through the virtues and the gifts / Kevin Vost.
      p. cm.
    ISBN 978-1-933184-41-8 (alk. paper)
    1. Virtues. 2. Christian lifet— Catholic authors.
3. Thomas, Aquinas, Saint, 1225?-1274. I. Title.
    BV4630.V67 2010
    241'.4 — dc22

                                 2009029094

To Eric and Kyle:
two talented young men

Contents

Acknowledgments

Many people helped inspire this modest tome. I thank you all, and I'll name just a few. This book would not exist if Dr. John Barger, Publisher of Sophia Institute Press, did not have the faith in my talents to let loose yet another writing project. I hope he'll be well pleased (or at least sufficiently so). Mr. Todd Aglialoro, editor extraordinaire, went far beyond the call of duty in transforming the abstract and nonmaterial ideas of our active intellects into the paper and ink that you hold in your hands. I thank as well the reader of *Memorize the Faith!* who emailed me a couple of years ago, asking where he could read more detailed accounts of the virtues and their parts. I've lost your name and email address, my inquisitive young benefactor, but my answer to you now is — *right here!* (Please feel free to contact me again.)

Mr. Shane Kapler is a dynamic young Catholic writer, the author of *The God Who Is Love: Explaining Christianity from Its Center.* He read an early draft of some of the first chapters, praised the best lines, and did not comment on the worst. (Todd usually gives those the ax anyway.) Others who've encouraged and inspired me to write again due to their support of my previous efforts include Tarek Saab, author of *Gutcheck: Confronting Love, Work, and Manhood;* Nick Alexander, musician and comedian, "The Catholic Weird Al"; Catherine Adamkiewicz, author of *Broken and Blessed* and writer for Johnnette Benkovic's *Canticle Magazine*; and Mrs. Johnnette Benkovic herself, who has featured my previous books on her *Abundant Life* program on EWTN. I also thank that fireball of energy and enthusiasm, Mr. Matt Swaim, producer, who has provided me the honor and privilege of speaking time and again to Brian Patrick of EWTN and Sacred Heart Radio's *Son Rise Morning Show*.

Closer to home, Mrs. Katy Yeley, tireless promoter of *Fit for Eternal Life* to all (including her Episcopalian women's exercise group), has shown enthusiasm for this book that has fired up my own. Mrs. Patti Moffett gave me encouraging feedback after reading my first try at the chapter on charity (among the first I wrote). She has been my running partner for one year and my "level three" friend for eleven.

Almost lastly, none of my books would exist if Mrs. Kathy Ann Vost did not possess all the talents required to keep our family and household thriving as I sit, and read, and think, and type. She always inspires me to make the most of my talents.

My gratitude also goes out to *you*. Thank you for reading. I hope you'll find it worthwhile.

Okay, lastly, I also thank God for providing you all.

Kevin Vost
Springfield, Illinois
Eve of the Feast of Corpus Christi
June 13, 2009

A Tale of Ten Talents

" 'Master, you have delivered to me five talents; here I have made five talents more.' His master said to him, 'Well done, good and faithful servant; you have been faithful over a little, I will set you over much; enter into the joy of your master.' "

Matthew 25:20-21

We're about to put on some very old, yet very powerful spectacles to take a fresh look at the magnificent parable of the talents. With modern lenses we tend to look at the parable in terms of making the most of the special gifts and talents God has given us. But when we view this parable through the glasses that the early Fathers of the Catholic Church passed down to St. Thomas Aquinas, we can see even deeper into the heart of things, all the way down to the lessons that apply not just to you *or* me, but to you *and* me, to *all of us*, to every member of humanity, made as we are, in the image of God.

Explanation aplenty will come in the pages ahead. But before we put on our glasses, please turn on your *imagination*, go back two thousand years or so, and picture the scene of the original parable in your mind's eye.

Long Ago, in Fruitful Lands

Long ago, in a beautiful haven of fruitful lands, nestled within the dusty sands of the ancient Middle Eastern landscape, a prosperous gentleman, preparing for a long and arduous journey, called three servants before him. He entrusted each man with a portion of his wealth, having divided it among them according to what he determined was each man's ability. To even the least able of the three, he presented an entire "talent."[1] Another servant received

---

[1] A talent was a sizable sum of money worth over fifteen years' wages for a laborer in those times. For the ancient

two talents, and to the most able of them all, five talents were given. Off the master went, entrusting his wealth to the care and judgment of these three men.

Do you recall what the master found upon his return? The man entrusted with five talents worked with them. He traded with them and produced five more for his master. The man with two did likewise, presenting his master with four talents, not two, when he came home. The master was quite pleased, of course. He told them how happy he was that they had been so faithful in caring for "a little," and that he would set them over "much."[2]

But why did the third servant raise his master's ire? Had he squandered the money on wine, women, and song? No, he had not. Had he gambled it away? By no means. In fact, he returned to the master the very same talent he had been given, after he had unearthed it from the hole in the ground that he had dug for its successful safekeeping.

And how exactly did the master react? You may recall that he took that talent from the servant and gave it to the man who had ten — "for to every one who has will more be given, and he will have abundance, but from him who has not, even what he has will be taken away" (Matt. 25:29).

Wow! Does this sound a little harsh to you? Is this another case of one of Jesus' "hard sayings"?[3] Let's look a little more deeply at the

Greeks, a talent of silver was the amount required to outfit one complete ship of war.

[2] If you'll recall the worth of even one "talent," you'll begin to appreciate the wealth and generosity of this master, for whom even five talents, over seventy-five years' worth of a laborer's wages, was but "a little."

[3] Compare with John 6:60 for the Apostles' reaction to the initiation of the Eucharist.

meaning of this parable, since it provides the principle that the rest of this book will build upon (and I hope you'll find it of interest).

The parable of the talents (described here according to Matthew's rendering, but also presented in Luke 19:11-27) is very rich, not just in talents, but in meaning, and at several levels. This parable relates far more than a tale of a master and his servants, of course. It tells the story of our relationship to God, to the "talents" he has given us, and to our rewards, both here on earth right now and later in the eternal heavenly kingdom.

The talents, of course, stand for far more than money. They represent all the good things God has given us.

So why was God so angry with the man who had buried his in the ground? Recall for one thing that the servant told the master he was *afraid*, because he knew the master to be a "hard man." He said that the master sows where he does not reap and gathers where he does not winnow. Hmm. Aren't we *supposed to* fear the Lord after all? I seem to recall that "fear of the Lord is the beginning of wisdom" and, indeed, one of the gifts of the Holy Spirit (Prov. 9:10; *Catechism of the Catholic Church [CCC]*, par. 1831). Further, the master was going off on some journey and expecting his poor servants to make him richer, through *their* efforts, upon his return. So was this servant really so far off base?

He most certainly was. We are to fear the Lord (and of course, to love him as well), not because of God's injustice and greediness, but for his infinite justice and boundless generosity. The fear should come into play in terms of our concerns lest *we* fail to uphold our end of God's most beneficent bargain.

My Talents Are Not Your Talents
Note well how the master dispersed different measures of talents to his servants, based on each man's abilities. We are all

unique human beings, with different levels of talents and abilities in different areas. There are significant individual differences in almost every human trait or capacity you can measure — verbal intelligence, musical ability, mechanical ability, mathematical ability, athletic ability, sociability, and on and on and on. And I think that these individual differences in interests and abilities are what makes the world go 'round (and what makes us so interesting to each other).

I hope at least some readers will agree that I've been given a talent or two for writing (worth, I hope, at least the price of this book). But you wouldn't want to hire me out as the fix-it man around your house. No, you might find yourself homeless after a while, as the walls came crumbling down around you over time. The same holds true with your car. Entrust its care and mainte-nance to *my* talents, and you'd be wise to invest in a bicycle before too long. (My own father, by the way, could have done either job quite nicely for you, and my wife and sons are pretty handy, too.) I'm sure you can catalogue some of your own talents (and lack thereof) as well.

When we appraise one another's abilities, we sometimes make overall assessments of a person's aptitudes or capacities. Despite the fact that every one of us has individual strengths and weak-nesses in particular areas, some folks do seem to be unusually tal-ented overall. They may be called the gifted, geniuses, superstars, innovators, movers and shakers, *sometimes even saints*, depending on their fields of endeavor and on just how far they exceed the norm.

Now, in our tale of the ten talents, we might see the man who was given five as the gifted superstar of the servants. He had the most "raw talents" given him by his master — and he ran with them. He made the most of them and produced the greatest results. The second man, with the two talents, was not so gifted, but he, too, made the most of what he had, and the master was quite pleased. The last man, with the least to begin with, did nothing to increase the modest measure with which he has been entrusted.

Hmm. What do you think the master would have done if the last had turned his one into two? Don't you suppose the master would have been as proud of this servant as he was of the other two? I think so. Consider for a minute another of Jesus' lessons. Our Master appreciates a poor widow's gift of two small copper coins, worth about a penny, more than the riches of a multitude, since she "has put in everything she had, her whole living" (Mark 12:41-44; Luke 21:1-4).

No, for this Master, it is not about the money. It is about making good use of the talents he has given us. Sure, some of us are better at some things than at others, but let's put these individual differences aside for a bit. The most important lesson of the parable of the talents, in my opinion, is not so much in terms of how we *differ*, but in terms of how we are *the same!*

My Talents Are Your Talents

Every last blessed one of us is endowed with a myriad of talents, with a host of robust powers, by virtue of our God-given nature as human beings. These are the common, universal powers of our human nature, of man's unique combination in the entire universe of a *hylomorphic* unity of body and soul (*hyle* being Greek for "form" or "spirit," and *morphe* being Greek for "matter" or "the body"). These God-given talents render us higher than the animals, although lower than the angels.

As Shakespeare declared of man with unrivaled felicity of expression:

Unearthing Your Ten Talents

What a piece of work is a man! How noble in reason!
How infinite in faculty! In form and moving how
express and admirable! In action how like an angel!
In apprehension how like a god! The beauty
of the world! The paragon of animals!

Hamlet, Act II, Scene 2, 310-321

Okay. Let's pay close attention now. It's time to cut to the chase. This book is about understanding and perfecting your highest human talents, your noble ability to reason, your amazing faculties of mind, your physical capacities for beauty of form and grace of movement, your ability to act angelically and to grasp and understand as is fit for a being who is made in the image of God (Gen. 1:26).

I use the term "ten talents" metaphorically you see, to represent ten virtues, ten perfections of our human powers. They include *seven natural virtues* which *we build* from the raw talents God gives us, and *three theological virtues* which we owe entirely to the *graceful gift* of God.

Three of these talents perfect the powers of our minds — our capacity to think and deliberate and understand and remember. Four of these talents perfect our capacity to control our passions, to calm our spirits, and to bring forth our best behaviors in our relationships with others and in our care of ourselves. The last three talents, the gifts of God's grace, perfect our relationship with him. When these last are allowed to flower, they inspire, form, and color all of our thoughts, feelings, and behaviors, as they relate to God, to our neighbors, and to ourselves.

Our tour of these talents will be guided first and foremost by the Angelic Doctor, the medieval philosopher and theologian St. Thomas Aquinas. Through his exercise of perhaps the most powerful gift of noble reason God ever bestowed upon a man, he studied, described, and prescribed, these ten virtues (*talents* in our terminology) more completely than anyone before or since. (He also did a most saintly job of living by them!) And believe me; the ten talents he describes are of absolutely invaluable importance to all of us today.

These ten talents yield the keys to spiritual growth through understanding our own human natures — body and soul. When we can come to understand ourselves, in our sensual animal natures, in our passions, in our wills, in our capacity to reason, and in how all these human capacities bear on our relationship to our Creator, we will find ourselves in the best position to make our talents grow. *The Master, you see, does not really reap where he does not sow; neither does he gather where he does not winnow.* The Lord has sown in all of us the seeds of greatness, but it is also up to us to see that they bear fruit.

Through our fallen human nature, it is oh, so much easier, and oh, so much more common, to live like that unfortunate servant who buried his talents under the ground. Poor Hamlet himself, after singing those praises of man's lofty potentials, moved right along to lament, "And yet, to me, what is this quintessence of dust? Man delights not me." This, of course, from the same young man who pondered the question: "To be, or not to be?"

Well, believe it or not, as providence would have it, ontology (the study of "being" itself) is among the metaphysical topics studied most deeply by St. Thomas Aquinas. And being, he declared (like the Lord in Genesis), is good, very good! Within these pages then, St. Thomas's golden wisdom on things anthropological and psychological (the nature of man and the human mind), as well as things ethical (the proper and highest of human behaviors), all informed by the theological (how it all fits into God's great plan for man and the universe), will guide us not just toward being, but toward being our best possible selves.

Let's move, then, to the introduction as I lay out our plan of attack, the attack against our fallen nature. To do so, we'll have to unearth some powerful ammunition — namely, those ten fundamental human talents that are all too commonly buried underground. We'll expose them to the light of day as we prepare to enter the fray, the battle to conquer our lower natures and let the best within us ride in triumph. When we've unearthed our ten God-given talents, the good in us will grow, so that we, our neighbors, and our Master, might be well-pleased.

PROFILES IN TALENT #1

The Talent of Humility:
St. Thérèse of Lisieux (1873-1897)

I wonder if, when reading the parable of the ten talents, St. Thérèse of Lisieux — the humble nineteenth-century Carmelite nun — compared her natural state to that least talented of servants. Could she have imagined that she would be revered one day as a Doctor of the Church, a teacher of great ethical and theological wisdom? When someone once told Thérèse that she was a saint, she rejoined, "No, I am not a saint, nor have my deeds ever been those of a saint. I am a very little soul whom God has overwhelmed with graces. In heaven you will see that I am speaking the truth."

Thérèse reminds us of the talent of humility. Aristotle's ethical ideal was the man of *megalopsuche* — the "great-souled" man: magnificent in achievement, wise, fair, courageous, self-controlled, and generous in sharing his talents with others. But the great-souled man (or woman) should be on guard, lest a great and overblown *ego* rear its ugly head. The Greeks taught that *hubris*, overweening pride, angered the gods.

Thérèse shows how spiritual greatness comes from humility, from realizing one's limits. An oracle once declared Socrates the wisest man in Athens, because only he realized how little he really knew. Or, as wise old Solomon put it, "Do you see a man who is wise in his own eyes? There is more hope for a fool than for him" (Prov. 26:12). Let us, then, strive to stretch our talents to the limits, but never to forget the limits of our talents, or the gracious Master who bestowed them upon us.

Unearthing Your Ten Talents

Introduction

On Growing Through Knowing

*"To know is a condition required
for moral virtue, inasmuch as moral virtue
works according to right reason."*

St. Thomas Aquinas

*"Restore the golden wisdom of St. Thomas . . .
spread it as far as you can,
for the safety and glory of the Catholic Faith,
for the good of society,
and for the increase of all the sciences."*

Pope Leo XIII

This book is about spiritual growth through understanding powers you might not even realize you possess. It's about building your God-given talents to their max. If you read carefully and prayerfully, follow along attentively, and ponder its lessons *after the book is closed*, then through the boundless grace of God and the peerless saintly guidance of St. Thomas Aquinas, you will come to know and understand the essential elements of your own human nature: of your unique mind/body unity, of the various and wonderful powers of your mind, and of the ten special virtues that will perfect your God-given capacities to think, act, and love.

You will thereby grow in your capacities to fortify your will, to improve your powers of reason, to curb your anger, to control your fears and anxieties, to live your life as a coherent whole, to treat your family, friends, and neighbors with fairness and love, to elevate your spirits, and to do honor to that Holy Spirit who dwells within you.

Thomas Taught Ten Talents

To unearth our talents, we'll need to do some digging. Fortunately for us, the ground has been broken, and excavated most fully, by none other than St. Thomas Aquinas. In his *Supplement to the Summa Theologica*, St. Thomas talks about the glorified resurrection of the body, and there directly addresses the parable of the talents in its relationship to man's abilities, his virtues, and God's grace.

Unearthing Your Ten Talents

St. Thomas Aquinas addresses several groups of virtues, the most fundamental of which can be grouped into the *three* virtues of the speculative or theoretical intellect, the *four* natural (or cardinal or moral) virtues, and the *three* theological (supernatural, or God-infused) virtues, thus yielding a nice, rounded *ten*, and leaving room at the end for that wonderful *eleventh talent* bestowed later by the Master himself. This enumeration and examination of these ten virtues (or, as we'll call them, *talents*), will serve as the fountainhead from which our understanding and application of our talents will spring. In this sense, this book is Thomistic. St. Thomas's own ideas will guide us, not only with regard to the ten talents, but with regard to our underlying human nature, which makes those ten talents possible.

And there is another sense in which we will strive to imitate St. Thomas in this book. As brilliant as the Angelic Doctor was, much of the light he bestowed on us was provided by the wisdom of the great thinkers who came before him, and he always told us as much. St. Thomas drew from an amazing array of Greek and Roman philosophers, from early Church Fathers, from earlier Doctors of the Church, and from the most perceptive and profound of the Jewish and Muslim theologians. (Indeed, in St. Thomas's *Commentary of the Gospel of St. Matthew* you will find a compilation of the commentaries of many early Church Fathers on the parable of the talents itself.)

In the pages to come, we, too, will profit from the golden wisdom of those holy and talented men, and indeed from some holy and talented women as well, recognizing and applying truth wherever it may be found: in St. Thomas's own writings, in Aristotle, in Stoic philosophy, in wisdom literature and other books of Sacred Scripture, and even in modern psychology and cognitive psychotherapy.

On Understanding Human Nature

To make the most of our talents, we must first know ourselves. We must understand our own human natures in terms of those special powers that set us above the other animals. Before we investigate the ten talents, and how we can build them and apply them in our daily lives, we will learn about how they arise from the depths of our human natures as *hylomorphic* beings; that is, unities of body and soul.

These talents arise from the very nature of our mind/body unity, in the way that our senses bring us information from the outside world, in the way that our minds can come to understand this information and examine it in the light of reason, providing the power for us to control our own actions (and even our feelings) in ways impossible to any other creature.

What is the nature, then, of the *human mind* and of the *human soul?* The answers we come up with will have great implications regarding to what extent we can enhance our own powers and unearth our talents.

Some famous moderns who have attempted to plumb the depths of the human mind have unearthed all kinds of "dirty" things that might just as well have been left buried. The Freudians said that deep within man lies a cauldron of seething passions. This *id* would rein over us, if it were not (barely) restrained by the fragile *ego* and the culture-bound restraining niceties of the *superego*. But way deep down, the *id* is us. Why should I, then, says Freud, be my brother's keeper? He would just as soon do me harm. *Homo homini lupus*, Freud declares: "Man is wolf to man." (Would that Dr. Freud had read St. Thomas's treatise on charity!)

Now, Christians know that none of us is without sin. Because of the Fall, we all are prone to sin and imperfection, although this was not our original intended state. We can experience lust and hurtful anger and a myriad of other impulses to sin, but through Jesus we can receive the grace to overcome them. We need not live out our lives at the level of our sin and weakness. Christians know that the violent, lustful, selfish *id* is not *really* us. St. Thomas Aquinas knew all about fallen man's sinful side, but he was certainly no Freudian pessimist regarding human nature. He was not so interested in how low we can go, as in how high we can rise. When St. Thomas digs deep into human nature, he's not digging for dirt, he's digging for *treasure*; and that's why he is the best guide for helping us unearth our talents.

So, in the chapters ahead, we will learn about St. Thomas's psychology and anthropology — his study of the nature of the mind and of the nature of man. We will learn about the "layers of the soul," the powers of external and internal sensation, the appetites and the will; and how these powers can be placed under the sway of our intellectual soul and God's grace, helping us to fashion these raw abilities into ten invaluable talents.

On Making the Most of It

Why do we want to understand human nature? So we can make the most of it. This is the practical benefit of spiritual growth through self-understanding. As we progress through the chapters of this book, we'll not only hear what St. Thomas and company had to say about human nature and each talent, but we'll also uncover practical tips on how to apply them in daily life *today*.

Mastering these talents will improve your life in many areas, by helping you:

• Improve your powers of reasoning, enabling you to weigh the truth in everything from scientific reports to advertising copy to claims of religious innovation;

• Focus your mental and physical energies on the things most truly valuable in life;

• Make order of your busy life so that your activities will blend into a meaningful whole;

• Curtail tendencies toward pessimism and hypercriticality;

• Attain greater serenity and stability in your moods;

• Realize which things are within your power to change, and what things you must leave in the able hands of God alone;

• Improve your capacity to restrain (and when necessary, properly express) your anger;

• Enhance your ability to apply discipline and self-control in your diet, exercise, and all important areas of your life;

• Develop a plan that will allow you to grow day by day in your faith and knowledge of God;

• Enlarge your capacity to love God, your neighbor, and yourself, and to show gratitude to the Master by willingly sharing your talents with others.

Profiles in Talent

Here's one more feature. When the ancient Greek historian and philosopher Plutarch wrote his *Parallel Lives* of famous Greeks and Romans, his intention was to instruct his readers in moral perfection by using inspirational biographical examples. Good idea, I say! Why not do the same here, fleshing out some of our key concepts with examples of famous Christians who embodied a particular talent in some special way? (And if you've read my previous books, you've already guessed that, like old Plutarch, I will include some famous Greeks and Romans as well.)

You've probably already read the Profile in Talent on St. Thérèse, and after this very paragraph, we'll take a look at a fabulously intelligent Greek, the man who laid the groundwork that made it possible for St. Thomas Aquinas to build his exposition on human nature, its gloriously potential talents, and how we may perfect them.

PROFILES IN TALENT #2

Overflowing Knowing:
Aristotle (384-324 B.C.)

"All men by nature desire to know." So wrote Aristotle in the first line of his *Metaphysics*. This is illustrated, he said, "through the delight we take in our senses."

Aristotle knew that we grow as human beings through our knowledge — knowledge of the outside world and knowledge of ourselves. In fact, when St. Thomas expounds on the first seven of our talents, he will borrow heavily from Aristotle, to whom he affectionately refers as "The Philosopher" in his writings. St. Thomas, however, had access to knowledge unknown to Aristotle: the knowledge of Christian revelation. This allowed him to go much further down the road to knowledge, all the way to heaven, through the knowledge of the Triune God.

Keep reading along, and your knowledge of Aristotle, St. Thomas Aquinas, your own human nature, and your untapped talents will continue to grow.

Part I

The Talents of Learning

"The intellectual virtues are about those things whereby a man is made happy; both because the acts of these virtues can be meritorious . . . and because they are a kind of beginning of perfect bliss, which consists in the contemplation of truth."

St. Thomas Aquinas

Chapter 1

Understanding . . . Understanding

"What is known in itself is a principle, and is at once understood by the intellect; wherefore the habit that perfects the intellect for the consideration of such truth is called understanding, which is the habit of principles."
St. Thomas Aquinas

"Understanding denotes a certain excellence of knowledge that penetrates in the heart of things."
St. Thomas Aquinas

Understanding is the first of three interrelated and hierarchically arranged intellectual virtues, the others being *science* and *wisdom*. I have classed these virtues under "the talents of learning." My dictionary says that to learn means "to gain knowledge, comprehension, or mastery through experience or study." Knowledge (science), comprehension (understanding), and mastery (wisdom) parallel quite nicely the three intellectual virtues that we'll address. All three are indeed acquired by experience or study, and all three are talents we must strive to develop if we are to perfect ourselves in God's image.

Two Forms of Human Goodness

Aristotle noted long ago that "goodness has two forms, moral virtue and intellectual excellence; for we praise not only the just but also the intelligent and the wise" (*Eudemian Ethics*, II, ch. 1:19). Every one of us has both rational and nonrational elements of our human nature. The talents of learning — understanding, science, and wisdom — belong to our rational nature. Our reason seeks out *truth*. The talents of living — temperance, fortitude, and justice — belong to our nonrational nature; to the realm of our appetites and desires. Our appetites seek out *the good*. But to attain what is *truly* good, our appetites must be guided by reason, through the operations of the will.

Reason, then, operates not only in its own speculative or theoretical realm of discerning truth in our minds, but also in the practical realm of guiding our actions and moral behaviors. This blending is embodied most directly in the last of our talents of living — that of prudence, the use of right reason as a guide to *right action*. For seeking what we see as good with all of our hearts and souls may in fact lead us down the path to destruction, if what we see as good is really evil. If we are to discern truth from falsity, good from evil, and return true profit to our Master, we must develop the talents of the minds.

Penetrating to the Heart of Truth

St. Thomas tells us that understanding is "an excellence of knowledge" that "penetrates into the heart of things." Our senses are the starting point of this knowledge: knowledge of the outside world, of ourselves, and even of God — as we see his attributes reflected in the wonders of Creation. But the senses are limited. They tell us only about the individual, particular things we see, hear, taste, touch, or smell. Animals have senses, some more acute than ours, but they do not achieve understanding. The "light" of their sensory capacities lacks the power to discern underlying commonalities and truths. They cannot discern general truths or universal principles from their sensations, *but we can*, through the power of understanding. Understanding allows us to penetrate deeper than outward appearances to inner essences, to fundamental principles.

This works on a simple level, based on our experiences in the outside world. When we see dogs, for instance, we don't just see particular noisy, furry, panting things. When we meet our neighbor's puppy for the very first time, we instantly classify it as a member of the abstract category of *canis familiaris* (all right, *dog*). Our intelligent minds are able to get at "the heart" or essence of what it means to be a dog, and we can distinguish a dog in an instant from a tree, or even a cat.

Of course, if you allow your understanding to function at this level all day long, then you're just "doggin' it." The human talent of understanding goes much further.

Understanding the Human Soul

To lay the groundwork for our understanding of understanding, and indeed of all the talents, we must recognize how, according to both Aristotle and Aquinas, we are composites of body and soul. It is not merely your eyes or brain reading this book, nor your disembodied soul: it is *you!*

Our bodies are plain enough to see. But what exactly is the soul? According to Aristotle, the soul, at its most basic level, is *the principle of life*. It is the "form" of the body, transforming it from inert matter to living being. We see that the Latin term for "soul," *anima*, carries on in modern English. Living things are *animate* (ensouled) creatures, while nonliving things (without a soul) are *inanimate* objects. So the first thing the soul does is make us alive. But let's take a look at what else it can do.

The Multilayered Soul

Biology 101 (or simply living on earth) teaches us that there are different levels of life with increasing degrees of complexity, capacity, and function. There are things that plants can do, by virtue of being alive, that rocks cannot do. My dogs Peppy and Mindy can do many things that the maple tree in the front yard can't, such as go for a walk. And, with no offense intended to Peppy or Mindy, you and I can do things that they could never even think of. Peppy could not read this book, for example, even with a T-bone steak as his reward. (And it's not that I haven't tried.)

This is all common sense, so far. What is not so common is the way St. Thomas explains the implications of the various powers of these three kinds of souls: *the vegetative soul,* which animates plants; *the sensitive soul* of the animal kingdom; and *the intellectual soul,* found only in man. Our human souls possess the powers of all three; for example, the vegetative's powers of growth and reproduction, the sensitive's powers of locomotion and sensation, and the soul's highest power, belonging only to the intellectual: understanding.

So, back to sense perception. Let's take a look at how the data brought to us through the powers of the sensitive soul make possible the uniquely human capacity for understanding.

THE ROAD TO UNDERSTANDING

Level of Soul	Power	Product
Sensitive	External senses	Sensation
	Common sense	Perception
	Imagination Memory Cogitative sense	Phantasm (or image)
Intellectual	Agent intellect	Abstraction
	Possible intellect	Idea (or concept)

Sensation

When we encounter some object in the outside world, we apprehend its features by one or more of the external senses that operate through our bodily organs. Through our eyes, ears, tongues, noses, or skin (and the primary brain areas to which their nerve endings project) we see colors, hear sounds, and so forth, and this experience we call *sensation.* The thing itself in the outside world is a composite of matter and form. As Aristotle notes, "Our sense organs detect the forms of these material things without the matter, like the impression of a seal on wax."

Perception

Have you ever heard the phrase "the sixth sense"? Well, according to Aristotle and St. Thomas, we actually have a total of *nine* "senses" — so to speak. It is at the level of *perception* that the first of a fascinating group of four "internal senses" comes into play. For human beings, the raw data from our five physical senses is merely grist for the mill of our experience. The four additional senses have no external sense organs of their own to receive information directly from the outside world; rather, they build and operate upon the information supplied by the five external senses.

Common Sense

This is not the "common sense" that your grandparents valued so highly (and rightly so). What Thomas called the *sensus communis* refers not to down-to-earth, homespun practical wisdom, but to a *general* or *overall* sense, as contrasted with the five *particular* external senses. Our particular senses bring us various separate feels, tastes, odors, sounds, and colors. These would be of little value to us without a higher-order common sense that can combine, integrate, and "make sense of them," if you will. Let's consider an example.

I feel dampness, taste a hint of saltiness, smell an unpleasant odor, hear a flapping sound, and see a patch of mostly white. What is it? My external senses have told me little else. All right, now I perceive that the object is a couple of feet tall and a foot or so wide, is oblong in shape with several tubular projections extending downward and one extending horizontally. It is just a foot or so away from me, is moving from side to side, and stops every few seconds, only to start up again. What is it now? Still don't know? Well, fortunately you have not actually *had* these sensations. I've merely described for you what I've sensed and perceived when our dog Peppy last came in from the rain and shook himself dry right in front of me.

The common sense combines and integrates the information from the particular senses, building from color, sound, odor, taste, and touch things such as size, shape, movement, and time. Ultimately, it is the common sense that allows us to perceive as *one* thing (Peppy in this case) the *many* data detected by the particular senses. In modern psychological terminology, the external, particular senses produce *sensation*, while the common sense produces *perception*. Perception derives from the Latin word *percipere*, "to seize wholly" (as a whole, i.e., *one* unified thing).

The common sense also perceives *our own operations of sensation*. For example, through the common sense we perceive not only the color and light emanating from the dog; we also become *aware that we are seeing it*. The common sense, then, perceives not just colors, sounds, tastes, smells, and feelings, but also our own processes of visual, auditory, gustatory, olfactory, and tactile experience. As St. Thomas said, "Neither sight nor taste can discern white from sweet: because what discerns between two things must know both. Wherefore the discerning judgment must be assigned to the common sense" (*Summa Theologica [ST]*, I, Q. 78, art. 4).

The common sense has one more very interesting trick up its sleeve. Partly because of its capacity to perceive not only objects, but our own sensory operations, it can also tell the difference between what we actually sense and what we merely imagine. For example, have you ever realized you were dreaming while you were dreaming? If so, your common sense was at work. Common sense can do this because of its unique situation, lying between the five bodily senses and the internal sense of *imagination*, coming to you right now.

Imagination

You are now reading the word *cow*. What's going on now in the world of your conscious experience? Because *you* are human, and *I* am quite confident about the Thomistic description of human mental powers, I'm willing to bet that you "saw" in your mind some kind of a stored visual image of a cow (assuming that you were not also looking at a real one at the time).

Aristotle's term for these mental images is *phantasm*, which derives from the Greek word for "light," and emphasizes the power of *visual* images. If you've ever heard, smelled, or touched a cow, or tasted one's milk, perhaps those impressions came to mind as well. Phantasms (images) need not be only visual, although the visual tend to be the most striking.

Phantasms allow us to call to mind things we have previously perceived, after they are no longer acting upon our external sense organs. They help free the rest of the intellectual powers from the confines of the immediate present. Indeed, the Philosopher (Aristotle) says, "The soul never thinks without an image" (*On the Soul*, III, 7).

Like the common sense, imagination possesses an additional intriguing capacity. Phantasms usually represent for us things we have perceived before, but we also possess the capacity to combine elements of previous sense impressions into *brand new*, purely "imaginary" objects. From our previous encounters with cows and with birds, for example, we can construct an imaginary winged cow (although I recall that when I was a child, my father often said we should be thankful that cows don't fly!).

Memory

The inner sense of *memory* builds upon the power of imagination. Through both, we retain impressions of objects previously detected by our external senses. In both, we have the capacity to reproduce those impressions at a later time. But memory has important additional powers. In acts of memory, we become aware not only of previous sense impressions that are absent; we become aware that they happened *in the past*. So memory includes a *temporal* component that imagination alone does not.

For example, think about your favorite teacher and an image of him pops up into your conscious awareness. This phantasm, however, is not just a timeless, floating abstraction. You picture him *in the context of your own personal experience*, drawing from some actual past encounter, along with a sense of his place in the chronology of your own life (be it the recent or distant past). Finally, your memory of this teacher evokes more than simply your past sense impression. It also evokes some *feelings*, doesn't it — admiration, nostalgia, gratitude, fondness, amusement?

But there is yet more to the power of memory. Aristotle and Aquinas were careful to differentiate two distinct powers of memory. *Sensory memory* is shared by both man and the lower animals, and it refers to the ability to retain and recall past impressions. Because of memory's closeness to the higher intellectual powers, we alone, as humans, possess the memorial power of *recollection* (or reminiscence), whereby we can use our reasoning powers to *consciously direct our memory processes* as we try to recall some object or event from our past. (I refer you to my book *Memorize the Faith!* for all the details!)

Cogitative Sense

Animals and humans share one other inner sense — and it's a most vital one. Not only do we perceive things as having certain sensible qualities, but we also perceive whether they are *good* or *bad*, desirable or undesirable, useful or harmful to us. In animals this is called the estimative sense (*vis aestimativa*) or animal prudence. St. Thomas notes that the lamb senses not only the size, shape, color, sound, and smell of the wolf; it also senses the *dangerousness* of the wolf, which is not present in the information derived from the external senses alone. This estimative sense is the cognitive component of instinct. Even we humans are naturally attracted to or repelled by some objects before we have time to reflect upon them with our intellects.

In human beings, this important power, so crucial to the preservation of life, is also subject to guidance by the intellect. It is called the cogitative sense (*vis cognitiva*), or "particular reason." It is called particular reason because it is subject to guidance by the reasoning powers of the intellect (which we'll look at later), but its focus is on particular things rather than on universal concepts. As the common sense integrates the information from the five external senses, so does the cogitative sense integrate the information from the external senses *and* the higher-order internal senses of the common sense, imagination, and memory.

The Phantasm of the Operating Intellect

There you have it: a brief look at the internal senses. Now let us return to the road to understanding, in order to see these senses in action.

After our external senses produce *sensation*, we separate the particular sense data and grasp what they represent as a unified whole. This is when our internal common sense comes into play; we saw that it is called *perception*.

We also form images or *phantasms* to retain the *percepts* (the products of perception: the mind's impressions of things as wholes) when they are absent, through the power of *imagination*, and when they are recognized as occurring in the past, via the *memory* — and we retain a sense of their positive value or threat to us through the *cogitative sense*.

All of these processes go on in some manner in all animal life. Useful as they are, they still stop short of the soul's capacity for understanding; they still refer to particular objects in the world rather than universal ideas. This is where the intellectual soul comes into play.

The Latin word *intellectus* derives from *intus* for "inside" and *leger* for "read": in essence, "to read what's inside." Our intellectual powers dig deeper than the surface appearances; they grasp the fundamental *essences* of the objects that stimulate our senses. This process has two major steps, and the first, *abstraction*, is the role of the *agent* (or active) *intellect*.

To abstract means to "draw forth." The agent intellect serves to draw forth from the phantasm, still enmeshed in all of the concrete particulars arising from the sensory data, its essential, universal nature. It strips the phantasm of its concrete particulars and reveals the essence of the object within. The agent intellect is said to "illuminate" the phantasm, shedding a special light upon it — like an x-ray that cuts through outer trappings to reveal what lies within.

Let's say I've heard and seen a very familiar noisy whiteness, which my common sense has told me is Peppy. He's in the next room right now, and I can't see him, but I can use him as an example because of his image or phantasm in my memory. A light goes off in my agent intellect, and I realize that not only is this Peppy, but he is one of a class of similar four-footed beings. I have abstracted or drawn forth his essence, common nature, or *quiddity* ("whatness") as a dog, disregarding the concrete, individual particulars unique to Peppy and not shared by all other dogs, like his proclivity for complacently lolling about outside during thunderstorms that send Mindy shooting straight down our bedcovers like a furry, shivering bullet.

This abstraction is immaterial. It is not a direct product of any particular sense organ. Although you know exactly what I mean by the word *dog,* we cannot see or hear or pet the universal idea or concept "dog," but only individual, particular real ones. The universal "dog" is abstracted from the phantasms, which derive from the internal senses via the external senses. Whereas the products of the senses deal only in concrete particulars, the abstraction is a universal that cannot be seen, heard, tasted, touched, or felt. An object of sense has now become an object of intellect.

But the intellect has not yet worked its full magic on that loud, fluffy whiteness that is Peppy . . .

The Possible Intellect and Understanding

Now we proceed to the fifth and final stage in the road to understanding. St. Thomas calls the abstraction produced by the agent intellect an *impressed intelligible species.* Wow! Now, there's a mind-stretcher. Let's work on this one. The term *species* refers to the mental representations of objects or things (like the percepts and phantasms we have encountered thus far) that we use as instruments of knowledge. Do you recall that the forms detected by the **senses** make an *impression* on the **sensory** powers like a seal on wax? Well, just as the internal senses create *expressions* from the phantasms or percepts, so does the *possible **intellect*** produce an *expressed **intelligible** species* from the abstraction produced by the agent intellect.

If this is still as clear as philosophical mud, let's wrap our senses (and intellects) around a little flow chart, so we can take in the whole shebang at a glance.

THE BIRTH OF AN IDEA
Thing or object

Faculties	Outer sense & Common sense ↓	Imagination Memory Cogitative sense	Agent intellect	Possible intellect
Product	Percept →	Phantasm →	Abstraction →	Concept or idea
Description	Impressed sensible species	Expressed sensible species	Impressed intelligible species	Expressed intelligible species

Adapted from, Robert E. Brennan, *Thomistic Psychology* (New York: MacMillan, 1941), 183.

Hmm. Still seeing this through a glass, darkly? All right, then, consider the *abstraction* of the agent intellect as the seed that brings forth the fruit of the idea or concept conceived in the possible intellect. The possible intellect is also called the *passive intellect*, because of its wonderfully flexible or plastic capacity to receive a virtually limitless array of impressions from the agent intellect. Sticking with our example, the possible intellect, having received the abstracted impression from the actions of the agent intellect, can now form an idea or concept. Now I see that the barking, furry, four-footed creature is not only Peppy, but a member of the species *canis familiaris* (all right again, *dog*). I can express this through language by calling him a dog.

At this point, I have achieved *understanding* (also called *knowing* or *simple apprehension*). I can also appeal to your understanding and expect you to understand me when I talk to you about my dog, even when you've never met him. Understanding involves more than giving universal names to concrete critters, of course. The human intellect can also come to know and understand abstract, immaterial entities such as truth, wisdom, love, virtue, God (in a limited sense), and indeed, even the workings of the intellect itself.

Further, through our capacity to see deeper into the heart of things than the superficial appearances of particular objects, to peer into the heart of their fundamental commonalities or essences, and to express these concepts in words, our capacity of understanding allows us to communicate truths to each other via true meetings of the minds. Differences in language pose no barrier, since the concepts that represent things share the same essences and can be translated across the globe. Neither are we limited by time, since we can read the thoughts of our predecessors and record our own for those who will follow us. No other creature on earth can do this. (Those who beg to differ will be hard-pressed to find evidence to the contrary in the academic libraries of the chimpanzees or dolphins!) A truly magnificent power is the uniquely human power of understanding!

So, we've had a look at the process of human understanding. Next, we examine understanding in the context of one of three perfectible "intellectual virtues" described by Aristotle and St. Thomas. You see, the Philosopher and the Angelic Doctor know that no human power will reach its full potential unless we purposefully practice it, hone it, build and perfect it, and this is the stuff of the virtues.

The Principles of Understanding

St. Thomas tells us that understanding is "a natural habit of the soul, whereby self-evident principles are known"(ST, II-II, Q. 8, art. 1). What are some self-evident principles that you and I can know, but our pets cannot? We know, for example, that the whole is greater than any of its parts. We know principles that Aristotle called "fundamental axioms," which lie at the foundation of human reason and cannot be denied without using them in their very denial.

Consider, for example, Aristotle's Law of Noncontradiction — namely, that "one cannot say of something that it is and that it is not in the same respect and at the same time." Ethical principles guiding human conduct include the precepts "Do the good" and "Avoid the evil." These kinds of fundamental principles are the starting points for all of the detailed chains of reasoning that take place in the talents of science and wisdom.

If we are to live morally, make the most of our talents, and please our Master, we must strive to employ and enhance this "natural habit of the soul." Fortunately, to this end the Holy Spirit has given us the *gift of understanding*.

The Gift That Flows from Faith

We've been examining the human power of understanding, as well as the human virtue of understanding. So what is the "gift" of understanding? And how is the gift of understanding different from the virtue of understanding?

St. Thomas tells us that whereas *human virtues* perfect our thoughts and actions *as moved by our natural reason* (a very important thing), the *gifts derive from God* and perfect our thoughts and actions *as moved by God*. God infuses them into our souls. We don't acquire them by our own powers; we need only to be open to receiving them and to use them. These higher, God-given perfections of our powers make us especially amenable to the promptings of God.

A full understanding of the concept of "talents," then, includes the virtues as *enhanced and transformed by the working of God's gifts*. Let's look now at the gift of understanding.

The gift of understanding flows from the supernatural virtue of faith (to be discussed in Part III, on the talents of loving) and is given to us to perfect human understanding. When illuminated by God's gift of understanding, our minds are enabled to grasp principles not only in accordance with human reason, but with God's divine and eternal law. Our understanding penetrates even deeper into the heart of things — the things of God. This applies both to the mysteries of the Faith — the gift of understanding can help us to work past the limitations in human cognitive capacity — and to practical principles of action and behavior in our daily lives. We cannot act in complete accordance with our religion, and attempt to live like Christ, if we do not understand what this entails.

Purity of Heart: The Beatitude of Understanding

Wonderful rewards flow from using our talents. In the narration of the Sermon on the Mount, beginning in the fifth chapter of the Gospel of St. Matthew, Jesus details eight "Beatitudes," or special blessings, that come to all who display perfections of various Christ-like talents: to the poor in spirit, to those who mourn, to the meek, to those who hunger and thirst for righteousness, to the merciful, to the pure of heart, to the peacemakers, and to those who bear persecution and reviling. Early Church Fathers related these Beatitudes of Christ to the various virtues, and in the pages ahead (using those Fathers and St. Thomas as my guide) I'll highlight how they are related to our talents.

"Purity of heart" is the beatitude that St. Thomas relates most directly to the gift of understanding, and this for two primary reasons. Here is Jesus' full rendering of the beatitude: "Blessed are the pure in heart, for they shall see God" (Matt. 5:8). This beatitude, like all the others, has two components, which Thomas lists as *merit* and *reward*. On the "merit" side of this beatitude is "purity in

29

heart," which means a freedom from inappropriate desires that leaves one's heart open to the holy things of God. We will see later that the virtue of temperance, or control of our appetites and passions, plays a vital role in this regard.

On the "reward" side, we see that God bestows upon those who devote their hearts to him the *vision of himself*. To see God is to see the source of all truth and goodness. Understanding denotes a kind of vision that "penetrates to the heart of things"; those whose hearts are pure can cultivate a talent of understanding that penetrates to the very heart of the universe, to the divine vision of God himself.

Faithfulness: The Fruit of Understanding

St. Thomas tells us that the Beatitudes promise rewards both here on earth and in heaven. Building upon St. Paul's letter to the Galatians (5:22-23), the Catholic Church has identified twelve "fruits of the Holy Spirit": "charity, joy, peace, patience, kindness, goodness, generosity, gentleness, faithfulness, modesty, self-control, chastity" (CCC, par. 1853). A modern translation of the *Summa Theologica* lists them as "charity, joy, peace, patience, longsuffering, goodness, benignity, meekness, faith, modesty, continency, and chastity" (*ST*, I-II, Q. 70, art. 3) — the same refreshing and delightful fruits, a few in slightly different verbal packaging.

St. Thomas, citing St. Ambrose in the first article of the same question, says these fruits "refresh those that have them with a holy and genuine delight." They are the results or products of virtuous deeds prompted by our receptiveness to the movements of the Holy Spirit. When we exercise our talents, both our natural virtues and the gifts of the Holy Spirit, the fruits blossom forth; and the fruit most closely related to the gift of understanding is the fruit of *faithfulness*.

Faithfulness is certitude about things unseen. When the virtue of understanding is perfected by the Holy Spirit's gift of understanding, its fruit is "the certitude of faith" (*ST*, II-II, Q. 8, art. 8). When we can feel certain of our faith, even with the awareness that the profundity of the mysteries of faith exceed the limits of our understanding while here on earth, we can truly experience that "holy and genuine delight."

The Foes of Understanding

Still, within this life, while we strive to deepen our understanding of the universe around us and of God's laws, we would also do well to be aware of the enemies of understanding, to unearth and expose these deficiencies or vices that darken the light of our understanding. Due to our fallen nature, it is so much easier for us to leave our talent of understanding buried under the ground. And in our modern, technological, media-saturated world, there are legions of diversions that can blind us to the wonders of God that surround us — leading to *hebetude of the senses.*

What the heck is "hebetude of the senses"? This is a fair enough question. It's not the kind of thing we're likely to chat about with a stranger on the elevator, once we've covered the weather. In fact, we're not too likely to hear much about "hebetude" in the Sunday homily either. Well, although the word *hebetude* has an archaic look and ring to it, our eyes and ears should still be able to recognize its sight and sound, so as to avoid it.

Hebetude derives from the Latin word *hebes* which simply means "blunt" or "dull." When we fail to develop our talent for understanding, our minds — the greatest and potentially sharpest implements God has given us — become blunt, dull, and unable to "penetrate into the heart of things." We render ourselves spiritual "dullards." We hamper our minds if we pay too much attention to the things of the body. We fail to realize our mental potential when we place too much emphasis on material things. We fail to achieve our angelic potential when we live too much on the plane of the animal. We fail to feed our intellects when we seek too much to feed only our senses.

There are many other ways that we can foster hebetude of the senses in ourselves, dulling our powers of understanding and setting poor examples for others. Do we feed our eyes with reality TV? Do we spend all our time reading simple romance novels or dime-store mysteries, leaving spiritual classics untouched? Do we sit mesmerized, chomping popcorn in front of the big screen, giving little regard to what we are allowing to play on the screens of the theaters of our minds? Do we know more about the lives of celebrities than we do about the lives of the saints? Are we too wrapped up in trivial phantasms of the senses to shine the light of our intellects upon profound ideas?

We should strive to build quiet sanctuaries in our own hearts and minds, where we can retreat to ponder higher things at times. (Still, when I go to the doctor or the dentist, I bring a good book — but I never think to bring earplugs!)

Sins such as gluttony and lust are also the enemies of deeper understanding. Gluttony for food can bring about hebetude of the senses, rendering us less willing and able to ponder things of the spirit, as our minds are directed elsewhere and our very brains are hampered by the sedating effects of excess food. Lust can bring about blindness of mind.

St. Thomas points out what most of us know from firsthand experience, that the stirrings of lust are even more powerful or "vehement" than the stirrings of gluttony, since their pleasurable rewards are greater. Food and sex are very good things when they are directed by the understanding of God's divine laws, but not when they are allowed to diminish or shut out that very light of understanding.

Understanding Underlies All the Unearthed Talents

St. Thomas tells us "the nature of each thing is shown by its operation. Now, the proper operation of man is to understand; because he thereby surpasses all other animals" (*ST*, I, Q. 1, art. 1). Understanding, then, is the most fundamental of our talents as human beings. The end of this chapter certainly does not bring with it the last word on understanding. We will see in the pages ahead how all of the talents are interrelated, together producing the wonderful treasures that will lead us to God. We'll seek to apply our talent of understanding to the principles at the core of all the other talents. And understanding itself will come up time and again, as a partner of knowledge, a component of wisdom, an integral part of prudence, and an outpouring of faith. It's time now to learn about science (also referred to as "knowledge"). It's not just for the folks with white coats and beakers, but for every creature made in God's image.

PROFILES IN TALENT #3

The Talent of Understanding:
St. Augustine of Hippo (354-430)

How is the Trinity reflected in the human soul? How are *memory*, *understanding*, and *will* the three parts of the human soul? St. Augustine addressed these sublime topics to help bring us to deeper levels of understanding of God and of ourselves.

St. Augustine's life was a journey to ever deeper levels of understanding. It was the *ad Hortensius*, the now lost book of the Roman philosopher Cicero on the benefits of philosophy, that drew the young Augustine to the love of wisdom. Still, as we see in his *Confessions*, his youth was marked by that blindness of mind produced by a lust for things of the flesh and of the world. It was not until he encountered Christ through the Scriptures that his eyes were opened to yet deeper levels of understanding. With his profound understanding of both the classical pagan world and the world of early Christianity, he came to see the deficiencies of the "city of man" and gave us a vision of *The City of God*.

St. Augustine was blessed with a brilliant mind that grasped the heart of the Scriptures and abstracted profound principles from the philosophy of Plato and Cicero. He provided foundational principles of understanding on which St. Thomas Aquinas was able to erect his magnificent cathedral of theological understanding. Open almost any section of the *Summa Theologica*, and you'll soon come across an instance in which St. Augustine has penetrated to the heart of things, to the benefit of *our* understanding.

Chapter 2

The Science of Science

*"A man forms a sure judgment of the
truth by the discursive process of his reason:
and so human knowledge is acquired by means
of demonstrative reasoning. On the other hand,
in God there is judgment of truth, without
any discursive process; by simple intuition . . ."*

St. Thomas Aquinas

*"In regard to that which is last in this or that genus of
knowable matter, it is science that perfects the intellect.
Wherefore, according to the different kinds of knowable
matter, there are different kinds of scientific knowledge."*

St. Thomas Aquinas

*"A characteristic of one possessing science
is his ability to teach."*

St. Thomas Aquinas

Every one of us has another intellectual talent that animals don't have: the ability to *reason*.

Angels don't need it. St. Thomas tells us that angels, being purely intellectual beings without bodily senses, achieve knowledge instantaneously through direct intuition. Most of our knowledge, however, is hard won over time, through the often-difficult, step-by-step processes of thinking. Aristotle's term for this special talent was *episteme*, from which epistemology, the branch of philosophy devoted to knowledge and knowing, derives. St. Thomas's Latin word for this talent was *scientia*, deriving from the Latin verb *scio*, "to know," and from which we get the word *science*.

So perhaps now you can see my dilemma in naming this talent, since either "science" or "knowledge" would work. I have gone with science as our chapter and talent title, in keeping with the language of St. Thomas, but please bear in mind that in the writings of Scripture, the *Catechism*, and the *Summa Theologica*, the virtue and gift of knowledge correspond directly to what we will call the talent of science. Let's find out exactly what it is.

In Aristotle's *Nichomachean Ethics*, we learn that whereas understanding is a grasp of *principles*, science is a matter of *causes* and *effects*. It produces comprehension of the causes of things. It involves *explanation*, rather than just *description*. It is knowledge of *why* things are, rather than just *what* things are. It requires both careful observation and logical reasoning. The subject matter of science in general is all of Creation.

Unearthing Your Ten Talents

In our day, a myriad of special sciences have been formed to investigate all sorts of areas of inquiry, with ever-increasing sub-specialization. Aristotle is considered the father of biology, and he examined all kinds of things. Over time, biology has divided itself into specialties and subspecialties: zoology, botany, herpetology, entomology, embryology, and genetics, to name but a fraction that come to mind. The other basic sciences, such as physics, abound in specialties and subspecialties too. All these specialties have their own specialized students or "scientists."

Yet how many of us would consider ourselves scientists? For even if we don't spend our time dissecting frogs or mixing things in test tubes, there is a real sense in which every one of us is a scientist, called to profit by building the talent of "science" (knowledge) given to us by the Master. When we apply our minds to comprehending the workings of the world around us, we do honor to its Maker, and we render ourselves better able to serve our neighbor and function in the world. Remember, the goal of all of the intellectual virtues is to arrive at truth.

The Scientist and the Schoolboys

Charles Darwin, having read the Philosopher for the first time, said the great names in the field of science in his time were "mere schoolboys compared with old Aristotle." Aristotle was the consummate scientist, not because he had the ultimate tools and technologies (he had next to none), and not because he made no factual errors (many are recorded in his writings), but because he understood the essential nature of science itself, and he applied it to its fullest.

When Aristotle sought knowledge of a particular subject, he, unlike many modern philosophers (and post-Reformation theologians), did not presume to start from scratch with his own interpretations.

Aristotle weighed carefully the theories and conclusions of thoughtful predecessors and then exercised his reasoning powers upon those opinions and upon the facts available to his own observation. Indeed, Aristotle himself made explicit those reasoning processes when he formalized rules of logic.

This systematized, formal reasoning had its predecessor in the discursive, dialectical, give-and-take series of questions and answers so gracefully displayed by Plato's teacher, Socrates, and Aristotle's teacher, Plato. Perhaps the ultimate example of dialectical and formalized reasoning, both in structure and content, is St. Thomas's *Summa Theologica*. (Indeed, after decades of immersion in modern atheistic/agnostic philosophers such as Friedrich Nietzsche, Bertrand Russell, and Ayn Rand, I myself came to see these modern thinkers as "mere schoolboys" — and a "schoolgirl" — compared with old Aquinas!)

But how can you and I *think* more like the Philosopher (Aristotle) and the Angelic Doctor (St. Thomas Aquinas)? Excellent question. Aristotle's writings on the specific intellectual virtue of knowledge are actually rather sparse, in comparison with the cornucopia of information he left us on the moral virtues we'll examine in Part II. Fortunately for us, St. Thomas has provided deeper insights into the talent of knowledge in his examination of the Holy Spirit's gift of knowledge.

Unwrapping the Gift of Knowledge

As we learned in the last chapter, the gift of knowledge helps us perfect the theological virtue of faith, so that we may believe the truths of God and his creation, and that we may see with our intellects and hearts what we cannot see with our senses alone. Understanding, St. Thomas tells us, gives us "a sound grasp of the things that are proposed to be believed." But science (knowledge) gives us "a firm and right judgment on them so that we can discern what is to be believed from what is not to be believed." In simple English, understanding says, "Yes, I get what you're saying," whereas knowledge says, "And I see that it is true [or false]."

Knowledge pertains to the relationships between all the things of God's creation, between their causes and effects. In the second quotation at the beginning of this chapter, St. Thomas notes that science perfects the intellect "in regard to that which is last in this or that genus of knowable matter." As obtuse as that might sound at first, St. Thomas, as usual, is perfecting sound common sense. We know things best when we know what is "last"; that is, their ends and purposes. Science, you'll recall, pertains to the reasons *why*.

Strengthening Your Knowledge

Thomas notes further that for different kinds of subject matter, there are different specific sciences. Let me, then, illustrate this understanding/knowledge distinction by proposing for your understanding a pair of principles derived from the specific field of anaerobic-exercise science (or physical strength training), since my mind has been wrapping around these kinds of principles for decades:

A. As one becomes stronger, additional sets of each exercise and additional exercises are required to stimulate further muscle growth.

B. As one becomes stronger, no additional sets of each exercise and fewer exercises are required to stimulate muscle growth.

Do you understand the principles proposed in A and B, at the level of simply grasping what is being said? Statement A implies that you must do *more* in terms of volume of exercise as you progress, while B states you must do *less*. Principles A and B conflict, don't they? So, given that we *understand* what is being proposed, how do we decide (achieve knowledge of) which is true? This is the sort of judgment that calls scientific thinking into play. Let's imagine how Aristotle or St. Thomas might approach the issue.

First, they would examine the "last things": the ends or goals or purposes. In our example, the exercises are being performed for the stimulation of muscle growth for size and strength. Next, they would examine what authorities have said about these principles, weighing these statements in light of their internal logical consistency and in light of their own observations of the facts (particularly the actual *results* of the training principles put into practice). They would seek out the reasons *why* the principles in practice seemed to work or to fail: they would seek out *cause-and-effect relationships*.

Perhaps statement A makes more sense intuitively. Lifting makes muscles bigger and stronger. The bigger and stronger the muscles get, the more work you'll have to do to make them even bigger and stronger. But remember that direct intuition is the province of the angels and, in the ultimate degree, of God himself. As humans, our knowledge derives through a sequential process of reasoning.

The Philosopher and the Angelic Doctor might ask, on a purely logical level, "If stronger muscles require more sets and more exercises, then is there any limit? If two sets are better than one and three are better than two, then are thirty-four better than thirty-three, and so forth, without end?" This is called an argument *ad absurdum*, drawing out the possibly absurd conclusions if the principle is carried out to its logical extreme.

But the practice of science involves more than logic alone. It requires observation. Our Philosopher and Doctor might examine formal research studies, if they existed, or try out the principles on themselves or others to see which actually bears muscular fruit in practice. Science often involves a process of comparison and judgment between different understood principles, in an effort to arrive at even deeper levels of understanding by finding true cause-and-effect relationships, and thus, true knowledge.[4]

Blessed Mourning: The Beatitude of Science

Let's move now from some mind/body considerations to a mind/spirit connection, as we see how the talent of science relates to its corresponding beatitude: "Blessed are those who mourn, for they will be comforted." How is mourning, a sadness or grieving, connected with discerning the truth? Good question. St. Thomas, of course, addresses it thoroughly (ST, II-II, Q. 9. art. 4).

Drawing from the wisdom of St. Augustine, we read that "knowledge befits the mourner, who has discovered that he has been mastered by the evil which he coveted as though it were

---

[4] By the way, here is my judgment on statements A and B. Statement B can be seen as the true one, when one understands the network of principles involved in stimulating and allowing for muscle growth. Stronger muscles do need greater challenges than weaker muscles to continue to grow, but those challenges come from increased *intensity*, heavier loads, not from increased *volume* (more and more episodes of loading). In fact, very strong muscles put great demands on the body's capacity to recuperate, and this is why the stronger you get, the *less* volume of exercise you actually need. You can do fewer sets (actually only one per exercise) and fewer exercises, in order to allow for recuperation and supercompensation (growing back stronger). (If you are interested in things muscular as well as spiritual, the actual principles of strength training are addressed in seven chapters of *Fit for Eternal Life*.)

good." Science, or knowledge, you'll recall, pertains to created things. Sometimes our judgments of causes and effects, of the true nature of things, will lead us to the discovery that what we sought as good was really quite the opposite. We may come to see that what we saw as beneficial to ourselves was actually harmful to self and neighbor (and perhaps offensive to God).

Knowledge, then, can form the basis of a healthy penitence, a penitence born of insight that leads to true remorse, to the sacrament of Penance, and to loving actions aimed at setting things aright. We should strive to become more aware of the causes and effects of moral messages and actions in the world at large and within the worlds of our own spheres of influence. We can ask ourselves if there are ways in which we support a popular culture that mocks religion, weakens the family, redefines marriage, and kills the unborn. What *effects* might our own actions, or even just our manner of dress or of speech, produce on those around us, for good or for evil?

And how about applying some scientific thinking to the *causes* of some of our own unsavory behaviors? Think back, if you will, to the last time you lashed out at a loved one. What were you telling yourself to rile your own emotions? (For *another person's* actions cannot directly produce *your own*.) Should we really walk around ready to fire back at the slightest insult or injury, after our Savior patiently bore so much more? Let's strive to become more "scientific" mourners, since we've been assured that God himself will comfort us.

Ignorance Isn't Bliss

Pop quiz! Do you recall that the vices opposed to the gift of understanding were hebetude of the senses and blindness of the mind? (Don't worry. If you didn't, you do now!) Well, the opposite vice of science is *ignorance*.

Aristotle once said there are many ways that an arrow can miss the target. If our target is to live in accordance with God's will, we'll also miss the mark if we don't bother to learn God's basic laws of archery. Ignorance in the spiritual sense, then, describes a lack of knowledge of the kinds of things we ought to know. As St. Thomas tells us, "we are all bound in common to know the articles of faith, and the universal principles of right, and each individual is bound to know matters regarding his duty or state" (*ST*, I-II, Q. 76, art. 2). If we don't seek out the knowledge of things we should know, this will indirectly produce sins of omission; when we fail to exercise our minds as we should and acquire knowledge of the basic truths of faith and morals, we will fail to do the good that we could. We will become deficient in how we perform our duties to God, neighbor, and self. If we fail to learn why an act is harmful and sinful, we are more likely to commit sins of commission, too. Ignorance is decidedly not bliss.

It's true that mourning, the apparent opposite of bliss, is the beatitude that arises when we dispel our ignorance about the pursuit of false goods. But from true knowledge comes a healthy regret that leads to the comfort of God, which is real bliss, once we have envisioned truer paths to follow. Those who have not achieved the beatitude of mourning may remain in what they think to be "bliss" as they pursue immoral or purely worldly goods, but these are false or incomplete goods that bring not bliss but its opposite.

Knowledge and Understanding:
Precepts Worth Sleeping On

The talents of knowledge and of understanding imply certain precepts: actions that not only follow logically from their nature but are also explicitly prescribed in the Old Testament. St. Thomas, citing the fourth chapter of the book of Deuteronomy, states there are three main things we should consider in relation to both knowledge and understanding: reception (learning and teaching), use (meditation), and preservation (memorization).

As for the *reception* of these talents, Thomas tells us this applies both to *learning* (our name for this group of intellectual talents, of course), but also to *teaching*. It is a well-known fact that one of the best ways to learn something is to study it well enough to teach it to someone else. So both learning and teaching can work toward reception of these gifts in oneself.

As for *use* of knowledge and understanding, this refers to meditation on those things we have come to learn and understand. We should ponder new truths, considering them both for their own sake and in how we can share their benefits with our neighbors.

Regarding the *preservation* of these gifts, this is the realm of the human memory. We are to retain and be mindful of the truths we have comprehended. We'll come across more on memory in this chapter's Profile in Talent, in the examination of the talent of prudence.

For now, let's just note a few passages from Deuteronomy 4 that St. Thomas cites to underscore his points on reception, use, and preservation: "These words which I command thee . . . shall *be in thy heart* . . . and thou shalt *tell them* to thy children . . . thou shalt *meditate upon them* sitting in thy house . . . *forget not* the words that thy eyes have seen and let them not go out of the heart all the days of thy life" (as cited in *ST*, II-II, Q. 16, art. 2).

Oh yes, and about this sleeping business: here is a very wise, simple, and psychologically sound recommendation from the Patron of the Schools himself. While explaining a statement from Deuteronomy suggesting that one might meditate upon the Law while asleep, he writes:

That precept of the Law does not mean that man should meditate on God's law by sleeping, but during sleep, i.e., that he should meditate on the law of God when he is preparing to sleep, because this leads to his having better phantasms while asleep, insofar as our movements pass from the stage of vigil to that of sleep . . . (ST, II-II, Q. 16. art. 2).

Modern psychological findings confirm this ancient recommendation to sleep on our problems, and to sleep shortly after pondering anything of importance. The mind tends to keep on working upon our last thoughts before sleep, according to a loose or "fuzzy" logic in which dream images will appear and associate in ways unimagined while awake. Done right before sleep, reading from spiritual materials, saying prayers, and examining one's conscience all help program our sleeping minds to operate on a deeper understanding of God's laws and his will. These are valuable methods of increasing our knowledge of our faith and of ourselves, and of enhancing our talents.

Time for Mass:
Please Leave Your Brains at the Door?

Have you ever heard a nonbeliever claim that Catholicism requires that we leave our brains at the door of the church; that we are expected to let the clergy, and ultimately the Pope, do all of our thinking for us?

Well, I've heard such statements, but I consider them a waste of sound waves!

Let's remember, for starters, that St. Thomas Aquinas, the very guy who is telling us all about *how humans think*, is the most esteemed and learned teacher of that selfsame Catholic Church! And indeed, for centuries now, pope after pope has been urging us to use him as the ultimate model of excellence in learning. He is the patron saint of scholars, after all.

Moreover, when applying our reasoning and interpretation skills to the Scriptures themselves, the Catholic Church has never encouraged anyone, not even a pope, to start from scratch, to make his own mind an ultimate authority over all who have gone before him. Consult the *Catechism of the Catholic Church*, for example, and you will see the workings of true science (in this case, the science of theology, the highest science of the things of God) at work. Note how for any given issue, the issue is defined, the Scriptures themselves are consulted, and the interpretations of the greatest minds in the history of Christianity are consulted as well. Interpretations are made by the Magisterium of the Church, and reasons are supplied for these interpretations. And all this use of the best of human reason is guided, as promised in the Scriptures themselves, by the inspiration of the Holy Spirit.

So, nobody is required to leave their brains at the doors of any Catholic Church. We are all encouraged to use our minds to their fullest for the glory of God, but we are also to avoid the kind of folly that presumes too much of the limited intellectual powers of any one of us, and at times, even of *all* of us!

This is why the Church speaks of the great "mysteries of faith" (which we'll consider further in chapter 8, on the talent of faith). No creature on earth or in heaven, not the greatest Doctors of the Church, not even the highest of archangels can fully grasp the mystery of their Creator. St. Paul told us as much: while here on earth we see but through a mirror dimly (cf. 1 Cor. 13:12). Humility, then, is the key to real knowledge.

The folly of presuming too much of our own intellectual talents is actually the vice most directly opposed, not to understanding or knowledge, but to that special amalgam of the two, and the highest of the intellectual virtues and of the talents of learning — namely, wisdom. So, after a brief tribute to the patron saint of scientists, we'll move along to ponder some words (and the talent) of wisdom itself.

PROFILES IN TALENT #4

The Patron Saint of Science:
St. Albert the Great (c. 1205-1280)

"A characteristic of one possessing science is his ability to teach," said St. Thomas, citing Aristotle, his great teacher across nineteen centuries. St. Thomas also had a truly magnificent teacher (and scientist, to boot) in his own time.

When Thomas was a young man, his classmates, taken in by his large frame and his reluctance to speak out, nicknamed him "the dumb ox of Sicily." Thomas's teacher, a German Dominican friar named Albert, had a deeper understanding of his young charge and told the lads, "Someday the bellowing of this ox will be heard around the world!" Indeed, in time, the ox's "bellowing" tended to drown out, to some extent, even the voice of Albert himself. Albert lived to enjoy that greatest joy of teaching: the full realization of the intellectual powers of one's most talented student.

Albert's knowledge of science was so great that some ignorant souls believed he was a magician, immersed in the occult. But Albert loved the study of nature because of the way it reflects the majesty and goodness of the God who created it. St. Albert also studied man and his talents. In his writings on the nature and perfection of human memory, for example, he painstakingly examined and explained all the rediscovered remnants of ancient Greco-Roman scholarship on the perfection of "artificial memory." Albert's writings on memory as a part of the virtue of prudence greatly influenced St. Thomas's writings on this subject.

Chapter 3

Words of Wisdom

*"By wisdom a house is built, and by understanding
it is established; by knowledge the rooms are filled
with all precious and pleasant riches. A wise man
is mightier than a strong man, and a man of
knowledge than he who has strength."*

Proverbs 24:3-5

*"Science depends on understanding as on a
virtue of higher degree: and both of these depend on
wisdom, as obtaining the highest place, and containing
beneath itself understanding and science, by judging
both of the conclusions of science, and of the
principles on which they are based."*

St. Thomas Aquinas

*"It is better to know a little about sublime things,
than much about mean things."*

Aristotle

"That means I want to know *everything!*"

That's what the man said. When I was going through my psychology doctoral program in the early 1990s, one of my most delightful and inspiring professors was a man who had completed his own doctorate while in his sixties. After a successful career in business, he had pursued his burning desire to learn about the workings of the human mind. One day he told the class that his true desire was actually to become a "polymath," which he said (tongue partially in cheek) meant that he wanted to know *everything*.

Well, we obviously don't have the time or the capacity to learn everything. We must set some priorities. After all, some things are far more worth knowing than others! Even loftier, perhaps, than the goal to learn about everything, is the goal to learn *everything we can about lofty things*. (We saw earlier that Aristotle thought so.) That's why, modifying a bit my professor's example, I like to think to myself now, "I don't want to know everything — just everything *worth knowing!*"

This ability to judge what is truly worth knowing is one aspect of the intellectual talent of *wisdom*, which we'll flesh out in the pages ahead. We will consider how the talent of wisdom relates to the talents of understanding and science, how the intellectual virtue of wisdom is perfected by the Holy Spirit's gift of wisdom, how the gift is related to the virtue of charity and the beatitude of peacemaking, how it is opposed by the vice of folly, and how we can strive to become wiser every day of our lives.

Science and Understanding:
Twin Pillars of Wisdom's House

Scripture tells us that there is both worldly wisdom and the wisdom of God (1 Cor. 1:19-21; Jas. 3:15-17). Although Aristotle lived before Christ, he believed in the wisdom of God. The laws of *science* examine physical causes and effects; the field of study that Aristotle termed *metaphysics* examines the fundamental causes that underlie them, including that ultimate cause of all effects, that unmoved mover that he called God.

This is why Aristotle called metaphysics the "divine science":

> The most divine science is also most honorable; and this science alone is, in two ways, most divine. For the science which it would be most meet for God to have is a divine science, and so is any science that deals with divine objects; and this science alone has both these qualities . . . such a science either God alone can have, or God above all others" (*Metaphysics*, Bk. 1, ch. 2).

Metaphysics, that which is above or transcends science itself, is one intellectual endeavor that seeks for an overarching *wisdom*. In Aristotle's scheme of the three intellectual virtues, science and understanding form the twin pillars that support the virtue of wisdom in its high place, from which it casts judgment on the conclusions of science and the principles of understanding.

Aristotle called wisdom by its Greek name, *sophia*, and we see that root in English words such as *sophisticated* and even *sophomore* (*sophia* + *moros*, a "wise fool" — perhaps a youngster who has acquired a little knowledge, but not yet learned its limits). And how about St. Thomas? The Latin for "wisdom" is *sapientia*, which we see, for example, in the biological term for the human species: *homo sapiens*. The capacity for wisdom, then, is a capstone of human nature, one of the loftiest things that lifts us higher than the animals, and closer to the angels.

How Many Scientists Can
Dance on the Top of a Pillar?

It seems to me that these days many a modern intellectual has abandoned the house of wisdom and set up his camp on top of but *one* of its pillars, like a modern-day secular St. Simon Stylites (a fifth-century ascetic who lived for thirty-seven years atop a small platform on a pillar!). By this I refer to *the worship of science*, and science in the restricted sense of "that which the folks with the lab coats, beakers, microscopes, and telescopes do." Some have called this *scientism*, a belief that science can address all questions relevant to human living. This is the view of science that feeds into the science-*versus*-religion debates, complete with bestselling books by scientists moving outside the fields of their expertise to attack religious beliefs (and believers) as gullible and puerile (if not insane and dangerous).

There are actually two fields outside their expertise that modern atheistic scientists wander into when they propagandize for worldly wisdom and deny that the wisdom of God exists. The first field is *religion* itself. Many set up ancient straw men to blow to pieces with their nuclear-era scientific arguments, because they lack both the knowledge and understanding of that which they attack. My heading here, mind you, is a play on the classic taunt that medieval scholastic theologians spent vast amounts of time and energy trying to figure out how many angels could dance on the head of a pin. (I've yet to come across this angelic dilemma in the *Summa Theologica*, although since angels are spiritual, rather than material beings, I doubt the scholastics would have thought that the question made much sense.)

Unearthing Your Ten Talents

To attack religion, scientists often enter a second field outside of their expertise. It is sometimes completely ignored, and it is most directly relevant to the intellectual virtue of wisdom. This field is *philosophy*, the very word meaning, "the love *of wisdom*."

Science can tell us how things work and whether we can control them. It cannot tell us whether we *should* control them. Science can tell us how to make bombs, but it cannot tell us whether and when we should use them. Science can tell us that human life begins at conception, but it cannot tell us whether it is right to end that life. Science is not self-reflective; it cannot judge itself. For this, we need philosophy. We need a field that looks at the big picture, that looks for reasons and meanings and purposes, as well as the causes and effects; that looks at what we *ought* to do, as well as what *can* do; seeking out what is true, and good, and beautiful.

We have seen that philosophy's realm includes the metaphysics that searches for ultimate truths. Science looks at material things with material causes and material effects. Metaphysics can ponder the spiritual realm as well. Among philosophy's other branches, it includes philosophical psychology (which we delved into in chapter 2 on the nature of the human soul). It also includes ethics, the study of how we can direct our behavior to the good (the stuff of the moral talents of living soon to be considered).

An over-reliance on science limits us to a worldly wisdom that God has made look foolish (1 Cor. 1:21). What else does "worldly" wisdom mean today? In terms of modern scientific thinking, the ultimate realities about almost anything in nature are usually presumed to lie in the world of subatomic physics. The world of psychology, too, tends to reduce things of the spirit to the realm of matter.

For example, why does a person think or feel a certain way? We can give psychological explanations that examine his beliefs and

attitudes, perhaps even tracing them to origins in family interactions in childhood, but many in the mental-health field today
believe that to be truly "scientific," we must dig deeper. We must
move from psychology to biology and chemistry, looking at the
brain, at its cellular structure, the functioning of the neurotrans-
mitters that transmit information among brain cells, and also at
the genetic information packed within those tiny cell nuclei and
mitochondria. Can we go further? We know that those chemicals
that act within the cells are made of molecules, the molecules of
atoms, and those atoms of subatomic parts.

But do these scientists miss the forest for the trees?

From Atomists to Thomists

Modern "atomists," "materialists," or "reductionists" believe
complex things, such as our own human thinking capacities, are
completely explained by reducing them to an understanding of
the workings of their smallest material parts. Of course, "there is
nothing new under the sun" (Eccles. 1:9). Such theories have been
around for a long, long time. Even in Solomon's day, there were
thinkers who said, "We were born by mere chance, and hereafter
we shall be as though we had never been; because the breath in
our nostrils is smoke, and reason is a spark kindled by the beating
of our hearts" (Wisd. 2:2).

We know now that those atoms and their parts are real, but are
they not the tiniest of saplings compared with the massive oaks of
our everyday human experience? And are they really even of the
same species? Scientists can weigh and measure atoms; they cannot measure thoughts, although thoughts most certainly exist (at
least, I *think* so).

A century ago, when the brand-new stimulus-response theories
inspired by Ivan Pavlov and his famous salivating dogs were taking

psychology by storm, fellow Russian psychologist Lev Vygotsky noted that trying to understand all the workings of human consciousness by the examination of discrete stimulus-response pairings is like trying to understand the relationship of water to fire only by separately studying hydrogen, which burns, and oxygen, which sustains fire. He did not think it wise.

And let's not forget, more than two thousand years before Pavlov observed that dogs can be conditioned to produce saliva when a bell has been paired with food (and his followers tried in vain for a few decades to show how this explains human thinking), we had Aristotle's depiction of just how intricate and unique is that human intellectual soul, whereby we, unlike any of Pavolv's dogs, can understand the concept of a "dog." We also saw how the *material* world and the *matter* of our own sense organs and brains provides the gist for an *intellectual* and *spiritual* mill that is the mind of man.

Divine Wisdom

Worldly wisdom, then, implies an understanding of principles and a knowledge of causes on a purely worldly, earthly level. The worldly wise might know how things work in the world, and how to use this knowledge for their own perceived advantage — for example, what brings them pleasure or money or the things they desire. They might even know how to get rich quick or how to win friends and influence people. Worldly wisdom, though, remains ignorant of a divine wisdom.

The divine wisdom that comes from God functions on a higher plane, seeking not only to know that A causes B and B causes C, but to know and understand Who created the whole alphabet of causes and effects, and what implications this might have for how we are to act in the world. Is there something ultimate that can fully satisfy our every desire? Is there a wealth that transcends money? What does friendship actually mean, and in what ways should we seek to influence people? What should we want them to do?

The love of wisdom that is philosophy, then, can serve as a training ground for true divine wisdom. Solomon said that "the fear of the Lord is the beginning of wisdom" (Wisd. 9:10). Metaphysics can show us on the plane of natural reason that there is a Lord to fear (i.e., respect and revere). With our hearts and minds open to examination of sublime and lofty things, we stand ready to receive God's revelation as well, and to live in accordance with his divine wisdom. Blessed with the benefit of revelation of the Scriptures as well as the observations of science, St. Thomas was able to take Aristotle's metaphysics and go even further in his consummate synthesis of natural and revealed *theology*: the study of God as reflected in all of creation and in his special revelation.

This is all quite lofty indeed. But wisdom, although one of the speculative or theoretical intellectual virtues, is not entirely theoretical. Wisdom is meant to be *used*. There is the practical wisdom called prudence, which we'll examine in Part II, but there is also a practical component to wisdom itself that Thomas elucidates in his writings of the gift of wisdom. Let's consider those words of wisdom next.

The Gift of Wisdom

The gifts of understanding and knowledge flow from the theological virtue of faith, but the gift of wisdom, the greatest of the intellectual gifts, flows from charity — the greatest of the theological virtues (1 Cor. 13:13). As with those other virtues, the intellectual virtue of wisdom is built by our own efforts and guided by human reason, but like God's other gifts, the gift of wisdom is infused in us by God. It "comes down from above" (Jas. 3:15).

St. Thomas further tells us that whereas the gift of understanding pertains to matters of perception, the gift of wisdom pertains to matters of *judgment*. This is how wisdom is practical: it contemplates divine things, and then "judges of human acts by divine things, and directs things according to divine rules." Here we obtain practical divine guidance for human ethical acts, from those pertaining to the unborn, to our duties to our families and our neighbor, and so much more. The gift of wisdom thus provides divine guidance in the actions of our daily lives. We might say that *if knowledge is power, then the gift of wisdom is heavenly power used only for the good.*

Indeed, "God loves nothing so much as the man who lives in wisdom. For she is more beautiful than the sun, and exceeds every constellation of the stars" (Wisd. 7:28-29).

Wise Are the Peacemakers

"Blessed are the peacemakers, for they shall be called sons of God" (Matt. 5:9). Thomas notes this beatitude "is fitted to" the gift of wisdom both in terms of *merit* and *reward*.

Peace refers to an ordered and harmonious arrangement, either within oneself, as when one experiences harmonious desires, or between the desires of others. The intellectual virtue of wisdom is conducive to peacemaking, because peacemakers obey reason. While peacefulness accompanies the theological virtue of charity, it is wisdom that produces the order that makes peace possible. Such is wisdom's work in the *merit* of the beatitude of peacemaking — exercising judgments in accordance with the divine will that produces peace and harmony, within and between men. Now, peacemaking's ultimate *reward* is to be called the sons of God, and we are called sons of God when we are like the Son of God, who was Wisdom Incarnate. By participating in wisdom, we become like sons of God.

Folly: Wisdom's Foe

Quoting St. Isidore, St. Thomas notes how *stultia* (folly) is related to the Latin word *stuporem*, a dullness, numbness, or bewilderment, from which we derive the word *stupidity*. Folly involves primarily *an apathy of heart* and a *dullness of the senses* relating to good judgment. The fool's heart does not reach out to higher things; his mind, therefore, lacks good sense, and he is prone to poor judgments.

The "wisdom literature" of the Old Testament is rife with pithy and penetrating comparisons and contrasts between the person truly wise in divine things and the fool absorbed in the things of this world. Let's consider but a sample from the book of Proverbs:

WISDOM VS. FOLLY

The wise person . . .	The fool . . .
loves you when you reprove him; grows wiser from instruction (Prov. 9:8-9).	rejects reproof and goes astray (Prov. 10:17).
listens to advice (Prov. 12:15).	is right in his own eyes (Prov. 12:15).
is cautious and turns away from evil (Prov. 14:16).	throws off restraint and is careless (Prov. 14:16).
is slow to anger (Prov. 14:29);	has a hasty temper (Prov. 14:29);
quietly holds it back (Prov. 29:11).	gives full vent to his anger (Prov. 29:11).

The wise person . . .	**The fool . . .**
sets his face toward wisdom (Prov. 17:24).	has eyes on the ends of the earth (Prov. 17:24).
finds wise conduct a pleasure (Prov. 10:23).	takes no pleasure in understanding, but only in expressing his opinion (Prov. 18:2).
attains honor in keeping aloof from strife (Prov. 20:3).	will ever be quarreling (Prov. 20:3).
lays up knowledge (Prov. 10:14).	repeats his folly "like a dog that returns to its vomit" (Prov. 26:11).

Note the assumed self-sufficiency of folly. The fool does not acknowledge the limits of his own judgment. He does not realize that ultimately "all wisdom comes from the Lord" (Sir. 1:1). Therefore, he is not amenable to correction or instruction — in his daily interactions with others, in his reading and study, or before the pastoral guidance of the Church. In fact, any attempt to reprove him or help him will meet with resentment and lashing out. Where wisdom is marked by restraint and patient delay in the expression of anger, folly lets it all out, right now, and is forever quarreling, forever babbling. St. Thomas notes that folly is also marked by insensitivity to its own consequences. The fool does not learn from his mistakes, but returns to them, as the proverb states so vividly, "like a dog that returns to its vomit."

And what is the main sin that leads to folly? St. Thomas, echoing St. Gregory the Great (and Proverbs), says that it is lust. Absorption in the most intense of worldly pleasures derails the mind from its pursuit of divine wisdom. We see this in Proverbs in the warnings against the adulteress and the harlot, and in the praise of the wise and virtuous spouse. We see this, too, in the book of the Wisdom of Solomon, with wisdom personified as a beautiful and virtuous woman, a divine gift to us from God. We must be particularly wary, then, of lust, lest it lead us to bury our talent of wisdom deep within the earth. As St. Thomas has said:

> Although no man wishes to be a fool, yet he wishes those things of which folly is a consequence, viz., to withdraw his sense from spiritual things and to plunge it into earthly things . . . The folly which is caused by a spiritual impediment, viz., by the mind being plunged into earthly things, arises chiefly from lust . . . (ST, II-II, Q. 46, art. 1-2).

Fortunately for us, St. Thomas has also given us some powerful practical advice in combating the passion of lust and in keeping our eyes trained on wisdom. (This we will see in chapter 5, when we unearth the talent of temperance.)

Eh, Wise Guy?

Did that subheading trigger any memories for you? If not, you must not be familiar with the ones we might call the Three Unwise Men. Yes, I'm talking about Larry, Curly, and Moe — the Three Stooges. Curly, you see, would blurt out this question whenever he was miffed at somebody, often the belligerently bullheaded and overbearingly bossy Moe, if I recall correctly.

The Three *Stooges* (please note the word's resemblance to *stultia* and *stuporem!*) are delightful representations of the *lack of* wisdom (for those who can tolerate their ballistic slapstick humor). It's as if they read the books of wisdom backward, or maybe upside-down. Please go back a bit to our wisdom/folly contrast, and note well how Moe was *always* right in his own eyes, going far astray into one disaster after another. He was totally unwilling to take advice from Larry or Curly — no, their offers of advice would almost certainly bring about hammers hurtling toward their heads. Indeed, it was because of Moe's unwillingness to take counsel that they developed their defensive side-hand block to counter his two-finger eye-gouging maneuver.

All three men were totally unrestrained and careless to the nth degree, with the hastiest of tempers and hairpin triggers unleashing the wildest of rage. They took no pleasure in understanding. They simply plunged into whatever the task at hand might have been, never seeking the least bit of knowledge as to how to accomplish it. Their eyes were on the earth, usually involving money-making schemes or helping some beautiful damsel. Only Moe felt entitled to unlimited expression of his opinion (and that often with his hands or fists, or whatever would-be weapon was lying around). To say that the Stooges were ever quarreling is an exercise in understatement, and they failed to learn, returning to disaster after disaster in every single episode.

Well, the Stooges were all in jest, but maybe we can all learn a little from their exaggerated examples on how to cut down on our own foolishness and how to truly become wise guys (and gals).

Words to (and from) the Wise

Solomon compares wisdom to a beautiful woman. "She is radiant and unfading, and she is easily discerned by those who love her, and is found by those who seek her" (Wisd. 6:12). Solomon said that he loved her and sought her from his youth, and became "enamored of her beauty." Indeed, "the Lord of all loves her" (Wisd. 8: 1-3).

How, then, do we come to love wisdom, become enamored by her beauty, seek her, and become wise? We need to cultivate the talent of wisdom through our own wise efforts, and we need to stay open to God's gift of wisdom as well.

Here are ten simple ways, if you'll take a look, that I've culled and collated from a very wise book.

- Fear and revere God, since "the fear of the LORD is the beginning of wisdom and the knowledge of the Holy One is insight" (Wisd. 9:10).

- Be receptive to reproof and correction, because if you "give reproof to a wise man . . . he will love you" (Prov. 9:8).

- Seek instruction, because if you "give instruction to a wise man . . . he will be wiser" (Prov. 9:9).

- Attune your senses to loftier things, "making your ear attentive to wisdom" (Prov. 2:2), and as for sound wisdom and discretion, "let them not escape from your sight" (Prov. 3:21).

- Watch your step! "Do not enter the path of the wicked, and do not walk in the way of evil men. Avoid it; do not go on it; turn away from it and pass on" (Prov. 3:14). "Turn your foot away from evil" (Prov. 4:27).

- Watch the company you keep! "He who walks with wise men becomes wise, but the companion of fools will suffer harm" (Prov. 13:20).

- Cultivate humility and "be not wise in your own eyes" (Prov. 3:3).

- At the same time, share of your wisdom. Don't hide it under a bushel basket (Matt. 5:15)! "Better is the man who hides his folly than the man who hides his wisdom" (Sir. 20:31).

• Exercise your talents of learning. "Blessed is the man who meditates on wisdom and who reasons intelligently" (Sir. 14:20).

• Don't forget to simply *ask* God for his *gift* of wisdom, since "if any of you lacks wisdom, let him ask God, who gives to all men generously and without reproaching" (Jas. 1:5).

Holding Wisdom in Your Hand!

As we conclude our introduction to the talents of learning, consider this last thought on the Holy Spirit's gifts of knowledge, understanding, and wisdom. Jesus told us that his Holy Spirit would guide the Church he founded upon the rock that was Peter. Recall, too, that all three intellectual talents are not purely speculative: they produce real results — things you can see, and yes, even hold in your hand! Whatever do I mean?

I'm indebted here to a modern Dominican, R. P. Thomas Pegues. In his *Catechism of the Summa Theologica*, Father Pegues makes the very wise observation that among the greatest of the Holy Spirit's gifts of knowledge, understanding, and wisdom are the *Catechism of the Catholic Church* and the *Summa Theologica* themselves! Where else can we obtain unparalleled depth of analysis and understanding of divine things, examined by the greatest intellects in Christian history, refracted through the prisms of both faith and reason, observable creation and divine revelation? Scripture itself has told us, "Do not slight the discourse of the sages, but busy yourself with their maxims" (Sir. 8:8). To truly unearth the talents of learning, then, every Christian would be wise to get busy — busy with the *Catechism* and busy with the *Summa*!

And next we must prepare to get busy ourselves — busy to move from the talents of our thoughts and ideas, to the talents of our emotions and behaviors; from the talents of the rational parts of our intellectual soul, to the talents of our nonrational appetites; from the talents seeking the true, to the talents seeking the good. Onward we go, then, from the talents of learning to the talents of living.

PROFILES IN TALENT #5

King Solomon's Gift of Wisdom

God spoke in a dream to King Solomon, son of David, and asked him what he desired. The young Solomon replied, "I am but a little child . . . Give thy servant, therefore, an understanding mind to govern thy people, that I may discern between good and evil . . ." (1 Kings 3:7, 9). God then said to him, "Behold, I give you a wise and discerning mind, so that none like you have been before you and none like you shall rise after you" (1 Kings 3:12).

An extraordinary wisdom was God's gift to Solomon. A well-known anecdote illustrates his wisdom: the tale of the two women who came before him with a baby whom each claimed as her own. Solomon's solution was to ask for a sword so that each woman might be given half. The real mother was known when she offered the child to the other, so that the child would not be killed.

King Solomon's gift of wisdom was also a gift to us. Some of the "wisdom literature" of the Old Testament, including Proverbs, Wisdom, and the beautiful love poetry of the Song of Songs (or Song of Solomon) has been attributed to him. Unfortunately, Solomon experienced a downfall in old age, when through the influence of his wives from foreign lands, he turned his heart from God and to their gods. It seems he experienced the folly he himself warned about that arises with too much concern with the world and the flesh. Perhaps he saw himself as no longer "a little child," but as "wise in his own eyes" (Prov. 26:12).

Part II

The Talents of Living

*"For a man to do a good deed, it is requisite
not only that his reason be well disposed by means of
a habit of intellectual virtue; but also that his appetite
be well disposed by means of a habit of moral virtue."*

St. Thomas Aquinas

Chapter 4

Forging Fortitude

"Fortitude is not lacking in courage,
for alone she defends the honor of
the virtues and guards their behests."

St. Ambrose

"Fortitude behaves well in
bearing all manner of adversity."

St. Thomas Aquinas

"Now, the brave man has a stronger love
for the good of virtue than for his own body."

St. Thomas Aquinas

The talents of learning perfect our human reason, that crowning glory of man that reflects our creation in the image of God. Of course, our job on earth is not only to comprehend the truth, but to *act* upon it. We saw that the talents of learning have practical applications. We cannot expect our actions to obtain good ends if we don't *know* which ends are truly good. Yet, unlike the mind of God, the mind of man cannot act on the outside world directly. We must work through the instruments of our bodies, torsos and limbs, brains and hormones, and all. And with our bodies come drives and desires; pleasures and pains. At times our desires for our own animal comforts and pleasures may conflict with what we know is truly right and good. We need, then, a set of powers that we can cultivate to bring our acts and behaviors in line with what we know is right, and that is why God has provided us not only with talents of learning, but with talents of living as well. We must strive to develop talents that enable us not only to perceive and judge what is true and good, but to obtain it: for ourselves, for our neighbors, and for the glory of God.

I'm sure you're aware that it can be one thing to know what is right and something completely different to get yourself to do it — or to know what is wrong and to keep yourself *from* doing it (Rom. 7:18-19)! Indeed, consider that even the demons believe in God — "and shudder," since their knowledge of truth does not bear fruit in righteous actions (Jas. 2:19). Some have argued that sin is merely a matter of misunderstanding or lack of knowledge, and that we will always seek what we believe is truly best for us, but how many of us can say this is true from our own experience? Come on now, have you ever known you really *should* do some difficult task, or abstain from some illicit pleasure, and avoided the task or pursued the pleasure anyway? If you have the same kind of human soul as I do, I'm willing to bet your answer is "Yes, and frequently so, indeed!"

Well, there is a group of talents just waiting to be unearthed that can help us acquire some inner harmony: to rein in our passions when they would lead us to evil, fire up our passions when they would leave good undone, keep us always mindful of the rights of our neighbor, and help direct all our actions toward that target of the good. Four in number, these "talents of living" have traditionally been called the *cardinal virtues*, since they "are about those things upon which human life is chiefly occupied, just as a door turns upon a hinge (*cardine*)" (*ST*, II-II, Q. 123 art. 7).

- *Temperance* perfects our capacity to seek what is truly good.

- *Fortitude* perfects our capacity to do battle with that which would keep us from the good.

- *Justice* perfects our capacity to seek and do good not only for ourselves.

- *Prudence* perfects our ability to determine the proper means to achieve the good and to act upon them.

These cardinal virtues have been addressed by the great pagan philosophers, including Plato, Aristotle, and Cicero. When the Greek and Roman Stoics argued that the chief goal of the truly wise man is to live a life of virtue, it was chiefly these virtues that they had in mind. The cardinal virtues come highly recommended in the Scriptures (see Wisdom 7:8, for example) and in the *Catechism of the Catholic Church* (pars. 1805-1809). They have been the subject of many a fine book, but nowhere else, to my knowledge, are they addressed as completely and masterfully as you will find them addressed in the second part of the *Summa Theologica*. We'll draw from the wisdom of all those sources, then, to see just how high those cardinals can fly.

The first of these talents of living is fortitude, that mighty "guardian of the virtues." Let's see what makes it tick so loudly and so forcefully.

The Talent of Fortitude: Guardian of the Virtues

Fortitude derives from the Latin word *fortis*, for "strength." Aristotle called this virtue *andreia*, from the Greek for "manliness," and implying valiance or bravery. Other common English words capturing some of the dimensions of this talent include *valor, courage*, and *endurance*. Fortitude is no virtue for the faint of heart. It is sword and shield for that spiritual warrior we all (male and female) are called to be. It faces down the difficult to protect the good.

Fortitude, you see, concerns "fear and daring." When we come under some form of attack, we may become fearful and withdrawn or enraged and aggressive, depending upon the circumstances and our own temperament. The talent of fortitude allows us to moderate our reaction appropriately; to overcome, as the case may be, undue fear or undue anger.

Here's how brave fortitude comes to "guard" the other cardinal virtues. Virtuous actions that serve the good must be consistent with the truths discerned by our reason. This is the job of that composite of intellectual and moral virtue called *prudence* that we'll consider more fully in chapter 7. Once we have determined the prudent, reasonable actions in a given situation, we must strive to establish them in human affairs — out in the real world. This is the province of *justice* (the talent of chapter 6). But in order to implement justice, we must not be taken off track by obstacles that could block its implementation. Perhaps we are lured off the path of justice by some illicit pleasure. This is a job for *temperance* (as we shall see in chapter 5). But if we are blocked from the implementation of a virtuous activity by some obstacle, by something difficult, painful, or fearsome, this is when the guardian virtue of fortitude comes to the front line of battle. Fortitude is the virtue that endures or attacks the obstacles that would impede or thwart the other virtues.

Fortitude can be seen in many simple ways in our everyday lives. We exercise fortitude, for example, when we defend our Catholic beliefs from those who question them, when we defend the right to life when the conversation around the water fountain has turned to such things, by speaking out and acting for the rights of the poor or the disabled or the elderly, by arguing against the harmful messages saturating our popular media, with the full realization that the herd is made uncomfortable by the one who dares to stand alone. We exercise fortitude when we do the difficult to achieve the excellent, by studying a few more hours rather than watching that movie, by lying down on an exercise bench instead of on the couch, by facing all the risks and difficulties that come with choosing parenthood. Fortitude is rough and tough. In a way, you could even say that fortitude is a "mean" thing. Let me show you what I "mean."

Moral virtues, such as the cardinal virtues, represent what Aristotle called "golden means," or states in perfect balance between deficiencies and excesses. When, for example, the passion of anger arises, true fortitude (along with the other cardinal virtues) would ensure that the anger be expressed at the right time, in the right measure, toward the right object, and for the right reasons (to help and not to harm). Aristotle called the virtue of the appropriate management of anger what we would translate as *gentleness;* anger's excess being reflected in the *irascibility* of the hair-triggered hothead, and its deficiency (in a person who is not angered by things that should provoke some measure of anger) by the rarer state of *spiritlessness.*

Consider this scene, if you will. Imagine that the magnificent Temple of Jerusalem, the House of God and monument to his greatness and glory, still stands.

You, with limitless power at your fingertips, walk in and find it full of money-changers, complete with their sheep and oxen. What would you do? Better yet, as they say, WWJD (What Would Jesus Do)? Of course, thanks to the twenty-first chapter of Matthew's Gospel, as well as the second chapter of St. John's, we do, of course, know just what Jesus did! He flipped over the money tables, made a whip of cords, and drove them all out, chiding them for turning his Father's House into a den of thieves. And this from the God who is love!

Now, that was *fortitude* in action. Jesus showed anything but spiritlessness! The holy Temple was degraded. The virtue of worship was being blocked by physical obstacles, and Jesus bravely removed them. He even got angry, but only rightly and reasonably so. He did not become excessively *irascible.* He could have turned them into dust, of course, but his aggression was moderated to serve the good and to reprove, but to do no harm to the transgressors.

An Irascible Appetite for Fortitude

In our consideration of the talents of learning, we saw how understanding, science, and wisdom relate to the human intellect:

the rational, reasoning part of the human soul. The intellectual virtues, our talents of learning, perfect this part of our soul.

But there is another way that humans alone of all the animals are made in the image of God. This is the human *will*. We have the capacity to choose between different courses of actions based on the judgments of our intellects. Animals have no will, only *instincts*. But in common with the animals, we also share basic *appetites* and desires, due to the vegetative and sensitive elements of our soul. How we differ from them is that we have the capacity to bring our appetites under the guidance of our reason. It is in the realm of our choices, our desires, our feelings, and our actions that the will and the appetites come into play, and the moral virtues, our "talents of living" answer the call to perfect them.

Let's look at a fuller picture of the human soul, in both its rational and nonrational elements, by examining the natural virtues laid out by Aristotle, noting in particular which categories of human capacity or power they perfect.

Please note that prudence has both intellectual and moral characteristics, as we'll see in chapter 7. The intellectual powers also include the will, which is an intellectual and spiritual (nonmaterial) power unique to the human mind. It is also referred to as the *intellectual appetite*, because the will desires the good *as the good is understood by the intellect*. So, even though the will is directed by the intellect, since the will is a kind of appetite that operates through choices and actions rather than pure thought, its operation falls within the realm of the moral virtues, the "talents of living," rather than the intellectual virtues, the "talents of learning."

The concupiscible and irascible appetites belong to the lower, sensitive level of the soul, as they desire goods presented to the senses, although we, unlike the animals, have the capacity to bring them under the control of our reason. They, too, are perfected by the moral virtues, our talents of living.

THE NATURAL VIRTUES

Category	Power	Virtue
Intellectual virtues *Talents of learning*	Speculative intellect	Understanding Science Wisdom
	Practical intellect	Art[5]
Moral virtues *Talents of Living*		Prudence
	Will, also called intellectual appetite	Justice
	Concupiscible appetite	Temperance
	Irascible appetite	Fortitude

Do you see fortitude there at the bottom? As we work our way through the talents of living, we'll be moving from the bottom up. Note in this scheme how fortitude is classed as a moral virtue (it guides our *actions* in relation to obtaining the *good*, rather than strictly our *thoughts* in relation to the *true*, as do the intellectual virtues) and how it perfects the human "irascible appetite." So, without further ado, please brace yourself for a crash course on fortitude's relationship to the irascible appetite.

---

[5] Art, although a virtue of the practical intellect, has not been classified as a fundamental intellectual or moral virtue, as we'll discuss a bit in our concluding chapter.

As humans with sensitive souls, we have within us an appetite with passions or desires that lead us to seek to obtain the things we *love* and see as *good* for us. This is called the *concupiscible* appetite, deriving from Latin words for "desire," and the talent of temperance (next chapter) exists to restrain and order it according to right reason.

We also have within us an appetite with passions that lead us to strike out against the things we *hate*, things that we believe deprive us of the good. This is the *irascible* appetite, deriving from the Latin words for "ire" or "anger." St. Thomas points out that in the animal world, virtually all aggressive behavior within the same species is guided by this appetite and involves issues of food and sex (predation, fighting for food or territory, and competing for mates).

A predator, driven by its *irascible* appetite, will run the risk of injury or wasted energy expenditure in facing the defenses of its prey, which serve as obstacles to his *concupiscible* good — that good being his next meal! Animals of the same species strike out against each other when they are perceived as obstacles to each other's goods, when competing for the same piece of food, or for the same mate. In animals, this behavior is driven wholly by instinct; only in humans can reason come into play to regulate these irascible passions, and this is fortitude's job.

There really is a lot to fortitude, as you are soon to see when we address its parts and its relationship to the gifts and fruits of the Holy Spirit, the Beatitudes, and the sacraments. Let us begin with what St. Thomas called the extreme example of the virtue of fortitude in action, something that animals and their unregulated irascible appetites can never achieve: martyrdom.

The Fortitude of Martyrdom

Remember that the irascible appetite enables us to fight against that which deprives us of the good things we love and desire. Typically this includes threats to our life and health, but as we saw in the quotation from Thomas at the start of this chapter, "The brave man has a stronger love for the good of virtue than for his own body." The martyr (having made full use of his intellectual talents) sees fidelity to God as the ultimate good, and his supreme fortitude allows him to fight against the evil that would ensue if he allowed his own aversion to pain (and even death) to conquer his will to follow God. Thus, fortitude helps direct the irascible appetite toward greater, more arduous goods over lesser, easier ones.

Thankfully, few of us today will ever have to face the supreme test of the talent of fortitude, but "he that stands firm against great things will in consequence stand firm against lesser" (*ST*, II-II, Q. 123. art. 4). In other words, when we have developed a talent of fortitude fit to confront great and arduous tasks, our talent will be all the more able to handle smaller, although still-difficult virtuous deeds in our daily life, whether it be speaking up for our beliefs, enduring physical fatigue when helping out a friend with some task, or studying or praying instead of vegetating in front of the television.

Enemies of Fortitude:
Fearfulness, Fearlessness, Daring

Recall that moral virtues imply perfect balances or "golden means" in thoughts, feelings, and behaviors. Moral vices arise when that golden mean is under- or overshot, either through deficiency or excess. Let's apply this to the vices that oppose fortitude.

Fortitude applies to matters of fear and daring. A person deficient in fortitude, then, will lack in courage, which lack we would call fearfulness or cowardice. When called to defend or protect for some good cause, the fearful man will leave his talent for manly fortitude underground (and, we hope, out of the sight and mind of his enemy).

On the side of excess, there is more than one vice. Since fortitude (like all virtues) is to be guided by reason, and not all risks are reasonable, fortitude will sometimes require some degree of fear and holding back. The vice of fearlessness entails taking just such unreasonable risks — risks not proportionate to the end or cause.

A similar form of false fortitude, a vice of excess, is called *daring*. The daring individual may leap toward a dangerous situation, like the fearless, only to leap back when he actually stands face-to-face with it. There are times to boldly seek out obstacles to the good; for example, when a law-enforcement officer must apprehend a dangerous criminal or when a soldier must face an enemy in battle. A reasonable boldness is compatible with fortitude. The vice of daring implies acting not just boldly, but *rashly*, by exposing oneself or others unnecessarily to dangers without sufficient counsel or forethought.

The daring man, then, jumps into dangerous situations too quickly, without proper counsel and consideration. So his excessive zeal in facing difficulties is also an affront to practical wisdom. When faced with the hazardous situation into which he has leaped, he may carry on, if he is also fearless, but he may pull back when he sees the results of his rashness and fears to face the obstacle that he too eagerly placed in his own path!

Viewers of the old *Andy Griffith Show* might recollect the times when Deputy Barney Fife would throw himself headlong into dangerous situations, and then find himself shaking so badly he could barely load his gun with the single bullet he carried in his pocket. (Fortunately for Barney, Sheriff Andy, a model of true fortitude, always came through to save the day!)

So, there are fortitude and its opposing vices in a nutshell. Let's move now to what St. Thomas calls the "parts" of fortitude. Once you've seen their majesty, I'm sure you'll always want to keep these parts in stock.

The Parts of Fortitude:
More than Magnificent!

Did you know that the cardinal virtues (our talents of living) have parts? You do if you've read the *Summa* (or even if you've merely read my own *Memorize the Faith!*). Memory itself, you might recall, was actually a "part" of the virtue of prudence (which we'll address here in chapter 7). How is it that virtues have parts? Well, to answer that question, St. Thomas explains to us they have three kinds of parts: integral, subjective, and potential parts.

Integral parts of the cardinal virtues are other virtuous habits that are necessary for the full expression of the cardinal virtue. They are the "gotta haves." St. Thomas said they are like the walls and roof and foundation of a house. *Magnanimity, magnificence, patience,* and *perseverance* are the integral parts that form the house of fortitude.

Subjective parts refer to the various "species" or subject matters that are addressed by the virtues. For the virtue of temperance, for example, sobriety is the subjective part that regulates our desire for alcohol, and chastity is the subjective part that regulates our passion for sex. Fortitude, interestingly, is the only cardinal virtue that does not have subjective parts, since its single subject matter is always essentially one thing: the difficult or "arduous" good.

Potential parts, also called secondary or annexed parts, address related, but more restricted acts or matters that do not call forth the full power of the virtue. The potential parts of fortitude include *constancy, confidence, strenuousness, manliness,* and *security.*

Unearthing Your Ten Talents

When we examine the virtues in all their parts, we gain a wider sense of their true majesty. They give evidence of how we were "wondrously made" in the image of God. So let's take a closer look at that image, by examining the four integral parts of fortitude. First we'll look at the golden means of the parts of fortitude, as well as the fool's gold of vices that undershoot or overshoot them.

THE TALENT OF FORTITUDE: TREASURES AND COUNTERFEITS

Virtue or parts	Vices of deficiency	Vices of Excess
FORTITUDE	Fearfulness	Fearlessness Daring
Magnanimity	Pusillanimity	Presumption Ambition Vainglory
Magnificence	Meanness	Waste
Patience	Impatience Resignation	Subservience Pseudo-martyrdom
Perseverance	Effeminacy	Obstinacy

Magnanimity: An Affront to Humility?

Remember Aristotle's concept of *megalopsuche*, or greatness of soul, from the first Profile in Talent box? The Latin words for "great" and "soul" are *magnus* and *anima*. Greatness of soul, then, is *magnanimity*. The magnanimous man, we are told, walks slowly and talks with a deep, calm voice. He focuses on great things, and he needs scarcely anything. Detractors of Aristotle (or of Christianity) sometimes portray this great-souled man as something quite contrary to a model of Christian virtue — something like Nietzsche's disdainful *ubermensch* (superman), or Ayn Rand's self-absorbed "productive genius" heroes. The ancient Greeks were well aware of the vice of *hubris*, that overweening pride that angered the gods and led to tragedy. But properly understood, magnanimity is miles apart from the vices of pride and vanity, and is indeed, a far closer neighbor to *humility* than to hubris.

Further, magnanimity is about great honor — not seeking it from others, but in doing great and honorable acts for their own sake, not for accolades. Where fortitude strengthens us to confront great and difficult evils, magnanimity strengthens us to obtain great and difficult goods. If you've been paying close attention, this connection with obtaining goods might suggest that magnanimity, unlike fortitude, is actually a part of the concupiscible, rather than the irascible appetite. Indeed, this is the first point St. Thomas addresses on the issue. Let's yield the floor to the Angelic Doctor himself:

> Good and evil absolutely considered regard the concupiscible faculty, but insofar as the aspect of the difficult is added, they belong to the irascible. Thus it is that magnanimity regards honor, inasmuch, to wit, as honor has the aspect of something great or difficult (*ST*, II-II, Q. 129, art. 1).

The person of true fortitude can endure great hardship because he is great-souled, because his focus is on great things.

St. Thomas masterfully dispels any conflict between magnanimity and humility by calling to our attention both the divine and the natural elements of our humanity. We are given great and powerful gifts from God (such as the ten talents). We also have a fallen human nature, prone to sin. Magnanimity reflects our consideration of that divine spark within us, the recognition that we are greatly blessed by God and should use our powers for the greatest works of good within our capacities. "Be perfect as your heavenly father is perfect," said Jesus Christ himself (Matt. 5:48). The magnanimous man strives for this perfection.

Humility reflects the recognition of that weaker side of our nature. It recognizes that while we must always strive to do great things and to make ourselves perfect, we never fully achieve that state in this life. Further, when we express the virtue of humility, we recognize as well the *greatness of soul* that God has also provided *in our neighbor*. The truly magnanimous man strives for great and honorable things, and also wishes the same for his neighbor.

If only we could reignite today that beautiful amalgam of magnanimity and humility once embodied in the medieval concept of Christian knightly chivalry: of bands of brave men working together to accomplish great deeds, each man striving for the honor of his lady, his family, his kingdom — and of Christ and his Kingdom and his Lady. (Don Quixote, you see, was not entirely off his rocker. The virtues of chivalry were both humble and magnanimous ones, but virtue must be expressed in keeping with the needs and circumstances of one's own time and place in history!)

The magnanimous man's other characteristics reflect and complement his humility. He moves slowly, because he is not in a rush to accomplish many trivial things, but seeks, rather, to accomplish important things that require careful attention. Rapid, flitting speech befits those who are easily distracted and quick to quarrel, but the magnanimous man's slow, calm speech reflects his purposeful focus on a few things worth talking about with care. The magnanimous man is also beneficent, generous, and grateful. He does good deeds, uses his talents for the benefit of others, and gladly repays with interest the good deeds done to him. He has no time for complaining, and he loves virtue so much that he will never employ dishonorable means even to produce a great accomplishment.

Great Soul or Great Ego?

Magnanimity's vices of excess are *presumption, ambition,* and *vainglory. Presumption* involves an unrealistic overconfidence in one's abilities, a tendency to bite off more than one can chew, to try to achieve beyond one's capacity, leading oneself and others to harm. (The extreme form of presumption is even considered one of the sins against the Holy Spirit: assuming that we can earn salvation through our own efforts, without the grace of God.)

Ambition refers to seeking honor from others for one's own profit, or to seeking honors for traits or accomplishments one does not actually possess, or to seeking glory without striving to benefit others. Such are not the ambitions of the great-souled individual.

Finally, *vainglory* can involve seeking honor or glory for deeds that are not truly worthy of honor (consider how many of our modern celebrities, for example, are showered with fame and wealth for base and vulgar deeds), seeking glory from those who cannot truly recognize what is honorable, or seeking one's own glory with no respect to God. The magnanimous man, devoted to honor, has little time to worry about glory. And, as Cicero notes, the desire for glory or accolades from others "enslaves the mind, which the magnanimous man should ever strive to keep untrammeled."

The vice of deficiency contrary to magnanimity is *pusillanimity,* which derives from the Latin word *pusillus,* meaning "very little," "petty," or "paltry." In considering this vice, St. Thomas makes a direct reference to the parable of the talents:

> Pusillanimity makes a man fall short of what is proportionate to his power . . . Hence it is that the servant who buried in the earth the money that he received from his master, and did not trade with it through fainthearted fear, was punished by his master (*ST,* II-II, Q. 133, art. 1).

No, neither fortitude, nor its parts, are for the faint of heart.

As great as magnanimity is, there is yet much more to the magnificent virtue of fortitude. Indeed, magnificence itself is the next integral part.

Magnificence: Talents Are for Giving Back

Magnificence derives from the Latin word *magnus* ("great") and *facere* ("to make or do"). The virtue of magnificence, then, is about making great things, principally through proper expenditure of money. Consider, for example, the enormous outlay of money and effort made by entire communities to erect the magnificent cathedrals and basilicas of Europe. (One good way to appreciate their magnificence, and to get in a good workout along the way, is merely to climb the stone stairs to their tops!) Some of these colossal monuments to God's glory took longer than a lifetime to construct, those who began the work not even living to see the finished product.

Magnificence does not mean that we must strive to become rich; rather, that, like the servant with his talents, we are called to make great things within the limits of our resources. Most properly speaking, magnificence concerns areas of great outlay: a wedding feast being a classical (and scriptural) example. How does this bear on fortitude? Through fortitude we overcome undue fear of threats, so through magnificence we overcome fear of threats to our pocketbooks. Magnificence shows that we have no inordinate love of money, that we appreciate what God has provided us, and that we have trust in what God will continue to provide.

What are the vices contrary to magnificence? As magnificence is greatness in expenditure, *meanness* or stinginess is smallness in expenditure. The mean man will worry too much about guarding his treasures, and will hold back and render less than what's required to make something truly great. He forfeits the good of the magnificent work for the sum it would cost him.

Meanness is obviously a deficiency. So what is the excess opposed to magnificence? It is *consumptio,* consumption or waste. We might also call it extravagance, or ridiculous and ostentatious expenditure: great outlay for goods that aren't worth it. Perhaps a modern example is the tendency to throw incredibly expensive and elaborate parties for a teenager's birthday. I've been told there have even been TV shows glorifying such events (Thankfully, I haven't tuned in by accident. I'm not sure that I'd have the fortitude to bear it for long.)

Patience: How Fortitude Trumps Sorrow

Patientia is Latin for the ability to endure suffering and patience; as a part of fortitude, it describes our ability to endure suffering without becoming sorrowful or defeated. Patience also implies an ability to endure suffering produced from the outside, from the acts of another. Have you ever told someone, "You have the patience of a saint"? If so, chances are the saint-like one has endured with calmness and grace the annoying and bothersome behavior of another person — perhaps complaints, disrespect, or ingratitude from someone he was trying to help. Patience is essential to fortitude, for when we seek virtuous goods, we must often bide our time. Many pleasures come quickly and easily, while virtuous rewards may be a long time in the making, sometimes even a lifetime. It is patience that enables us to do the right things with gladness in our hearts, even while we endure present evils.

St. Thomas did not address specific vices opposed to patience, leaving us without his expert guidance in this specific instance. But perhaps we can exercise our own intellectual talents a bit to come up with some possibilities. If patience enables us to bear external hardships without sorrow, then vices of deficiency could involve fleeing from a situation of hardship or staying the course while suffering sorrow. Avoidance of the difficult situation or lashing out at a person producing a hardship might simply be called *impatience*. Enduring a hardship but giving in to sorrow and sadness describes the state of *resignation*. The resigned individual may bear a hardship, but in the spirit of defeat, as if having no other choice.

And how about vices of excess? Here are a couple of possibilities. As fearlessness entails a lack of reasonable concern for true dangers, what we might call *subservience* could represent a lack of reasonable concern for how the unreasonable demands of others hinder us in doing the good. The subservient individual does not try to avoid unnecessary entanglements and does not complain; in modern terminology, this might be called "doormat" behavior, allowing oneself to be needlessly stepped on and walked over by others. And as daring opposes fortitude by dashing headlong into dangers without forethought (and falling back through fear when the dangers are actually met), so, too, what we might call *pseudo-martyrdom* could represent willfully seeking out relationships with others or commitments of various sorts that present obstacles to our true good, and then complaining to others of the pains we must endure.

Perseverance: Fortitude Endures

Perseverance is a special virtue of fortitude that enables us to endure to the end in committing virtuous acts, regardless of delays. For a soldier, this might mean displaying the fortitude to stand his ground until the end of a long, drawn-out battle. To the magnificent man, this might mean staying the course and providing whatever additional funds are needed to fund a great public work beset with unexpected delays or expenses. To the student, perseverance might mean continuing to study until he's ready for the exam, even as the lure of the television or the mattress grows ever more enticing.

And in a grander sense, perseverance comes into play as we must continue to practice the virtues of faith, hope, and charity (to be addressed separately in Part III) throughout the course of an entire lifetime, for as St. Matthew tells us, "But he who endures to the end will be saved" (Matt. 24:13).

Perseverance moderates or controls our passions, such as fear of weariness or failure in the face of delays. As you might expect by now, its contrary vices would involve a deficiency or excess in this regard. The vice of deficiency in relation to perseverance carries the name of *effeminacy* (which does not mean that women cannot display perseverance — as we know for a fact that so many women saints have persevered so remarkably well despite the most trying obstacles and delays). Effeminacy refers to an inability to suffer hardship or toil due to an inordinate love of pleasure, play, or leisure. You've heard the saying, "When the going gets tough, the tough get going." Well, when the going gets tough, the effeminate get going, too, to look for something easier to do! The effeminate individual has trained himself toward weakness and delicacy. He has buried his talent for manly perseverance deep in the ground, where it may rest in peace, but fail to grow.

The vice of excess that opposes perseverance is called *obstinacy* or *pertinacity*, with related terms (courtesy of St. Isidore and Aristotle) being *impudence, headstrong, and self-opinionated*. The pertinacious will not back down or relinquish their beliefs or behaviors, even when shown to be wrong. Their goal is not virtue, but self-expression through recalcitrant vainglory.

Fortitude:
The Gift That Keeps on Enduring

The virtue of fortitude is a natural or human virtue. We can all train ourselves to regulate our irascible appetites with our reason in order to stand fast in the face of adversity and strive for the "arduous good." Indeed, fortitude was among the highest of the pagan moral virtues. But recall that the "talents" we are examining here are more than human virtues alone. They are human abilities and virtues enhanced and perfected through the grace of God.

Fortitude is one of the seven gifts of the Holy Spirit related in Isaiah 11:2 (listed as *might* in the RSV). It has a special relationship to the sacrament of Confirmation. The bishop calls on the Holy Spirit to endow the newly confirmed with these gifts so that they might persevere in the life of faith. But how does the gift of fortitude differ from the virtue of fortitude?

The virtue of fortitude notes a "firmness of mind" both in doing good and in enduring evil, especially when those goods and evils are "arduous" or difficult. Still, it is not within our human powers to obtain every good and avoid every evil, and we may be overcome by death. Human fortitude cannot always obtain its ends. By the grace of the Holy Spirit, however, man ultimately defeats even death by enjoying eternal life, so that *through God's gift of fortitude, we can actually achieve our final end of the most arduous and highest good*.

Further, St. Thomas tells us that through the gift of fortitude, a "certain confidence" is infused in our minds regarding this ultimate victory, exceeding what is possible through the imperfect virtue of human fortitude alone. Finally, while human virtues enable us to control our passions in conformance with *human reason*, gifts of the Holy Spirit enable us to control our passions in conformance with *the guidance of God*.

The *gift* of fortitude, then, surpasses and perfects the virtue of fortitude, since it both *comes from God* and *makes us more amenable to divine inspiration and prompting.* The gift of fortitude can strengthen us to endure tasks beyond our purely human endurance, as the holy martyrs would attest.

Blessed Are Those Who Bear Persecution

St. Thomas notes how St. Ambrose related fortitude to the beatitude of bearing persecution and reviling, which makes a lot of sense. The reward for those who bear persecution is "the kingdom of heaven," that arduous but highest of goods we just addressed when considering the gift of fortitude. St. Thomas also expands on St. Augustine's commentary on how fortitude relates to the beatitude of hungering and thirsting for righteousness, and this is a bit more subtle. Striving for righteousness (or justice) can involve the performance of difficult deeds, but even more difficult is to "hunger and thirst" with "an insatiable desire" to do them, despite the difficulties involved.

Fruits of Fortitude

Two fruits of the Holy Spirit flow from the gift of fortitude: patience and longanimity (the soul's capacity to endure long delays in the accomplishment of goods). These fruits relate to attributes within ourselves resulting from God's gifts. We should pause a bit now to ask ourselves how we can build our talent of fortitude, and what kinds of fruits it will bear in our daily acts.

What hardships might I endure today? Can I prepare myself to bear them gladly with fortitude? Will I show the patience to suffer hindrances from others without getting upset? Will I persevere if delayed? Will I strive to express my magnanimity? Will I think holy thoughts and strive to accomplish deeds worthy of the great soul God has given me? Will I retain a sense of humility at my own imperfection? What will I do today to honor and respect that kernel of greatness of soul that God has also given to my neighbor? What can I do to revive a sense of brave and noble Christian chivalry?

These are but a few questions we can ask ourselves as we prepare to examine next the talent perfecting another aspect of our human nature, that wellspring of human desire, the concupiscible appetite.

PROFILES IN TALENT #6

He Wrote the Book on Fortitude:
Marcus Tullius Cicero (106-43 B.C.)

Marcus Tullius Cicero, philosopher, orator, consul of the Roman Republic, and savior of his country, died too soon to know Christ, but he did seek God, and he did embody fortitude. Cicero's book *De Officiis* ("On Duties"), written as a guide for his son away at school in Greece, is a masterful exposition and practical guide to the classical cardinal virtues, including fortitude. He addressed these virtues and their parts in his works on public speaking and rhetoric, as well. (Cicero, you see, thought that a public speaker should understand and talk about virtuous things.)

I chose Cicero for this essay, not only as model of thinking about fortitude, but as a most lofty example of its actual perfection. Cicero was magnanimous and magnificent. His great thoughts on philosophy were cherished by St. Thomas, and the Founding Fathers of the United States were no strangers to his political theories. He left the most extensive and magnificent legacy of written material of any man from ancient Rome.

He also performed the highest act of fortitude. He was martyred for writing and speaking openly against the tyranny that brought the republic of Rome to its end. He patiently offered his neck when Marc Antony dispatched a soldier to bring back for public display in Rome the head that had dared to think and the hands that had dared to write against the reign of tyranny.

Chapter 5

Tempering Temperance

"It belongs to temperance to preserve one's integrity and freedom from corruption for the sake of God."

St. Augustine

"Since, however, man as such is a rational being, it follows that those pleasures are becoming to man which are in accordance with reason. From such pleasures temperance does not withdraw him, but from those which are contrary to human reason."

St. Thomas Aquinas

The talent of temperance really "hits us where we live" more than any other talent — if we consider "where we live" to be within our own bodies. As hylomorphic beings of body and soul, we have both physical and spiritual needs and desires.

Now here's a pop quiz from our Profile in Talent box on Aristotle. Do you recall why he argued that every one of us "desires to know"? Our desire to know is proven by "the delight we take in our senses." That is, how we love to see, hear, taste, smell, and touch good and delightful things. Through our senses, we desire to know truths, and also to acquire and experience things we believe to be good — especially things that look and feel good to us.

Animals, of course, have sensitive souls, and there is no mistaking their clear-cut desires. St. Thomas, remember, said that in the animal world, virtually all of the aggressive actions of the irascible appetite serve the purpose of acquiring food or sex, those primary goods essential to individual survival and to survival across the generations, by removing obstacles that stand in their way. This appetite *for* those goods is called the *concupiscible* appetite.

In animals, which lack an intellectual soul, these appetites operate automatically at the level of *instinct*. We do not make moral judgments on animal behaviors. Predators are not wicked. They are preprogrammed by their God-given natures to seek out their own goods for individual and species-wide survival. It is only in man that our concupiscible and irascible appetites must be put to moral use, under the guidance and direction of our reason and our will — that is, through the talent of temperance. Let's see how.

Temperance: Key to the
Kingdoms of Integrity and Freedom

The word *temperance* acquired a tarnished reputation in the twentieth century. The Temperance Movement achieved strict legal prohibitions of the sale of alcohol, from which the public rebelled. Later in the century, "If it feels good, do it!" became the popular mantra of enlightened selfish wisdom. If you argued for the virtue of temperance, you had to be prepared to be labeled a prohibitionist, Puritan, Victorian, repressed personality, or some other variety of sour-pussed party-pooper!

Well, much of the "party" that was the second half of the twentieth century has pooped out on its own and brought with it all sorts of personal and social hangovers. Freedom *from* temperance has bought with it all kinds of consequences, from increases in addictions, obesity, STDs, divorce, and that total eradication of a human being's freedom: legalized deprivation of the right to life and liberty through death by abortion.

Critics claim that temperance means, "If it feels good, *don't* do it." But this suggests a false dichotomy. What temperance really says is, "Always keep your pleasure-seeking in line with the dictates of reason; always keep your sensitive soul under the guidance of your intellectual soul." But that's not a pithy catchphrase, of course! How about, "If it *feels* good, *think* before you *choose* whether to do it"? For it is by applying *thinking* and *choosing* to the equation that we rise above the level of the animal appetite, and act fully like human beings, employing the capacities of *intellect* and *will* — those very capacities that reflect our creation in God's image.

St. Augustine said that temperance is the key to integrity and freedom. Temperance produces *integrity* within us, making us interiorly united, when it conforms sensual appetites to our reason and will. St. Augustine, like St. Paul before him, was well aware of times in his own life when those faculties within himself warred with one another, making him a kind of prisoner. It was only when he truly embraced his faith in God that he was able to attain temperance and enjoy the integrity and freedom that it brought.

Enjoying the Pleasures of Temperance

If we listen only to what the world says, and fail to exercise our intellectual talents of reasoning, we may easily come to picture temperance (as the world does) as some humorless Terminator-like being, seeking relentlessly to seek out and destroy any signs of fun and pleasure.

St. Thomas tells us this is just not so. *Temperance seeks not to destroy pleasure, but to remove our desires from the pleasures that would destroy us.* The pleasures we derive from eating, drinking, and sex were created by God and are therefore good — in fact, vital for survival. The virtue of temperance enables us to make the best possible use of these desires. Let's see how, by examining its parts.

THE TALENT OF TEMPERANCE: PONDERING THE PARTS

Integral parts	Subjective parts	Potential parts
Shamefacedness	Abstinence	Meekness
Honesty	Sobriety	Mildness
	Chastity	Continence
	Purity	Modesty

Temperance's Integral Parts:
Shame on You . . . Honestly!

The two integral "gotta have" parts of temperance are *shame-facedness* and *honesty*. How's that? Well, shamefacedness refers to the sense of shame; the fear of disgraceful deeds. Through it we fear physical and spiritual dis-integration through the unchecked passions of the concupiscible appetite. We fear the loss of spiritual freedom that comes from being enslaved by the body's desires. Shamefacedness, says St. Isidore, is "a fear of base action." St. Ambrose chimes in that it is also "lays the first foundation of temperance, by inspiring man with the horror of whatever is disgraceful" (*ST*, II-II, Q. 144, art. 4).

As much as the temperate man abhors the disgraceful, he is drawn to the truly beautiful, and one thing of great spiritual beauty is the virtue of *honesty*. *Honesty* derives from the word for "honor," and things honorable possess true excellence. The temperate man is characterized by honesty in that his internal thoughts and his external acts and deeds are consistent. Temperance thus keeps our intentions and actions clear. With temperance there is no need to hide them; in the words of the Stoic philosopher (and Roman Emperor) Marcus Aurelius, there is no compulsion "to lust after anything that needs walls and curtains" (*Meditations*, Bk. II, 5). And temperance keeps our desires in due proportion according to the dictates of our reason. St. Thomas even notes that according to the philosopher Plato, if we were able to see spiritual honesty with our eyes, it would "arouse a wondrous love of wisdom."

Temperance's Subjective Parts:
Eat, Drink, and Be Hilarious

Perhaps you weren't used to thinking of temperance in terms of those two integral parts, but the subjective parts have crossed the thoughts of all of us. Subject matters such as sobriety, abstinence, chastity, and purity deal with issues we all must face, and issues that for so many in our culture involve addiction and self-enslavement.

Through *sobriety*, we limit our desire for alcoholic beverages and their intoxicating effects. But remember that temperance does not remove us from all pleasures, only those that exceed the dictates of our reason (and thus are truly bad for us). Now, we tend to think (with good reason) of sobriety in terms of curbing the excess consumption of alcohol known as drunkenness. But remember that moral virtues are golden means between extremes of excess *and* deficiency. St. Thomas, in an intriguing passage, notes that it is indeed possible to miss the target of the virtue of sobriety through an error of deficiency. How's that? Well, "if a man were knowingly to abstain from wine to the extent of molesting nature grievously, he would not be free from sin" (*ST*, II-II, Q. 150, art. 1). Interesting, huh? But not inconsistent. St. Thomas tells us that God's creation is good, all of it.

St. Thomas warns us against excessive drinking that clouds our ability to reason, but has advised that when we drink, we should "drink to the point of hilarity" (or a friendly lightheartedness). It goes without saying that the proper time, context, and situation must always be considered. St. Thomas's wise and humane advice would never justify drinking that would put an inebriated person behind the wheel or put others at risk in any way. In exercising our talents, temperance will help us use and enjoy our appetites properly.

"Wine drunk in season and temperately is rejoicing of heart and gladness of soul. Wine drunk to excess is bitterness of soul with provocation and stumbling . . . " (Sir. 31:28-29).

(Although neither St. Thomas, nor the author of Sirach mention it directly, I can only assume, hope, and pray that the principles applicable to the fruit of the vine would apply in equal measure to the fruit of the barley and hops!)

The next subjective part of temperance relates to our desire for food. It is called *abstinence*, and its contrary vice is gluttony. I've addressed gluttony (which is one of the seven capital or deadly sins) along with practical suggestions to conquer it in my book *Fit for Eternal Life*. For our purposes here, let's just recall that when we develop the capacity for abstinence, for reasonable self-control in the domain of food, not only do we become better able to beautify and honor our bodily temples of the Holy Spirit, but we also build the capacity within ourselves to focus instead on the higher things of God.

Pure Passion

The last two subjective parts of temperance, *chastity* and *purity*, attempt to regulate the most powerful and vehement of human passions, that of sexual desire. Chastity refers to restraint in sexual intercourse and purity to restraint in related sexual behaviors, from things such as looks, to touch, to kisses. God built into us an urgent drive to reproduce, accompanied by the highest of earthly sensual pleasures. Before the Fall, this would have presented no problem, as man's intellect, will, and desires were aligned in the state of natural grace. Since that time, we've had a real battle on our hands. St. Augustine tells us that "the most difficult combats are those of chastity; whereas the fight is a daily one, but victory rare," and St. Isidore adds that the Devil subjects mankind more by carnal lust than by anything else because "the vehemence of this passion is more difficult to overcome" (*ST*, II-II, Q. 154, art. 3).

Vices opposed to chastity and purity on the side of deficiency or insensibility, are, as you might guess, quite rare. God made us as sexual beings. The urge to reproduce and the pleasure attached to the process are very powerful parts of our animal nature, and being in accord with nature, of themselves are very good. It is the rare individual who does not feel the pull of the concupiscible appetite, and the pull itself is a good, not a sinful thing. Of course, as humans, we are called to act not only in accord with our sensitive animal nature, but with our rational human nature, which must usually act to curb excessive desires or desires for inappropriate sexual relations.

Virginity and celibacy are not vices of deficiency, since they do not deny the good of sexuality, but forgo those physical goods for even higher spiritual goods. Perhaps the most likely vice of deficiency would involve a spouse who has no desire to participate in the normal sexual intimacy of Matrimony, when the couple has not decided to forgo relations for some length of time for some mutually agreed-upon moral reason.

Combating the vices of excess, this is the stuff that the virtues of chastity and purity are usually all about. Chastity itself derives from the word *chasten* or *chastise*, which implies restraint and correction. Everyone is called upon to exercise them in some manner, for even married individuals are called to reserve their willful sexual desires and behaviors for their spouses.

The main vice opposed to all manners of temperance in the sexual realm is, of course, lust. We have considered in earlier chapters its power to produce blindness of mind and to derail even the intellectual talents of understanding and wisdom. In the interpersonal realm, pure lust reduces another person into an object existing to satisfy one's own selfish desires. And even the man who sees the object of his lust as more than only an object and cares for her as a person, lust can blind him to the harm that illicit sexual behavior can bring to them both and to others around them. This is most clearly seen in some cases of adultery, for example.

If lust is allowed to reign unchecked, its possible manifestations in actual harmful and sinful behaviors are legion. This is why Jesus admonished us to bar lust even from our looks and from our hearts. When a man chances upon a beautiful woman, or a woman comes across a handsome man, it is no sin to realize and appreciate the fact of their comeliness, but to master the virtue of temperance, we need to leave it at that, and not dwell on, fantasize (remember our power for making *phantasms* or images?), or conjure up lustful *ideas* in our intellects. So, the next time you are struck by a person's physical appearance and might be tempted toward a lustful thought, why not start building the habit of sexual temperance by thanking God for crafting such beautiful creatures and saying a brief little prayer for yourself and that person.

So, what can one man or woman do to battle this lewd and lascivious legion of lust? Let's see what the Angelic Doctor himself would bid us do to win this war.

Thomas's Tip to Tackle Intemperance:
On Avoiding Sexy Singulars

The allure of pleasure being what it is, building the virtue of temperance is a long, tough battle. How are we to fight it? There are no easy answers, but St. Thomas does provide one simple, deceptively abstract-sounding yet exceedingly practical little line that can be a big help: "Hence, the most effective remedy against intemperance is not to dwell on the consideration of singulars" (*ST*, II-II, Q. 142, art. 3).

What is he saying? Why is it so profound?

Let's recall Aristotle's observation that "we all take delight in our senses." Well, the pleasures brought through the sense of touch are the most powerful of all, especially those we derive from eating and from sex. These are the driving forces of the animal, sensitive soul, and they operate upon *singulars* — real, particular things we can actually see, hear, or smell, prompting the desire to taste or to touch. As reasoning beings with intellectual souls, we realize that to let these desires run rampant would bring great harm to ourselves and to others, so we must regulate or temper them, and it is the power of the intellect itself that makes this possible.

Lust, the most powerful challenge to the virtue of temperance, thrives on singulars, especially visual images of particular, enticing bodies. Unfortunately, advertisers and the purveyors of popular media know this so well that we are under the perpetual bombardment of seductive visual images purposely designed to arouse our lusts, be it on television shows and commercials, in movies, in newspapers and magazines, or plastered greater-than-life-size on unavoidable roadside billboards. The styles of dress, attitudes, and manners of behavior they promote bear fruit in the attire and demeanor of real flesh-and-blood men and women. Males, by our natures, are especially prone to distraction by these visual images, both through the media and in daily life. What, then, are we to do?

St. Thomas would suggest that we focus on the opposite of those "singulars" — namely, "universals." Instead of turning the eyes and imagination on this or that particular woman, try the mind on "woman." Instead of lusting after a particular woman, try focusing on her identity as a "daughter," or "sister," and perhaps as someone else's current or future "wife" or "mother." The lustful man functions like an animal, at the level of the sensitive soul. He perceives singular bodies, and desires them, but does not strive to abstract the essence of the human souls within. Instead of emulating the Don Juan-like "lover" who lusts after singular women but does not really love them at all, emulate the man who shows true love for all women by honoring and respecting them.

Spouses blessed with the sacrament of marriage can treat each other with special loving attention as singulars. Indeed, St. Thomas wrote about the appropriateness of a wife adorning herself and striving to make herself attractive to her husband. Yet the married couple, too, should strive to love rather than lust, loving each other in the flesh, yet never seeing or using the other as mere flesh alone.

St. Thomas was especially adept at practicing temperance because of his focus on the very highest of universals, the divine things of God. Spiritual sloth, he wrote, paves the way for lust and intemperance, because "those who find no joy in spiritual things have recourse to pleasures of the body" (*ST*, II-II, Q 35. art. 4). To curb lust, then, let us focus most on the highest things of God, from which love, not lust, will flow.

Potential Parts of Temperance:
Meek, Mild, and Manly

The potential parts of temperance include meekness, mildness, continence, and modesty.

"Blessed are the meek," declared Jesus in the third beatitude. But what is *meekness*? As a potential, annexed, or related part of temperance, meekness refers to the moderation of anger. Anger, as Aristotle tells us, must be displayed in the right measure, at the right time, toward the right person, for the right reason. The temperate person carefully regulates and employs the use of anger, to correct his neighbor, as did Jesus, the personification of meekness, in his cleansing of the Temple. Note well here that the meek are not weak! We already saw how the Temple-cleansing embodied a most manly fortitude as well.

St. Thomas was well aware that the Roman philosopher Seneca described *mildness* or *clemency* as leniency of a person of superior

station toward a person of inferior station when inflicting a punishment, and as a temperance of the soul when taking revenge.
Cicero chimes in that clemency is a virtue whereby the mind is restrained by kindness when an unreasonable hatred for another has
arisen. So whereas meekness regulates the passion of anger, mildness or clemency regulates its actions of external punishment. The
vice opposed to mildness is cruelty, something a person with any
God-given talents should hold in the greatest disdain.

Of Donuts and Dresses:
Self-Control and Self-Display

Continence has much in common with the virtue of temperance itself, and is often confused for it. Let's consider a simple di-
etary example. There it is, and oh, how grand! Yes, it's a plump and
succulent jelly-filled Bismarck donut. As beautiful and tempting
as it is to me, instantly triggering my Pavlovian salivatory reflexes
(my mouth is watering), I resist the temptation and content myself instead with a mug of hot black coffee. I ask you: have I dem-
onstrated temperance, then, or continence? (The answer starts
with a *c*.)

Continence refers to the ability to resist evil desires within
oneself. Surely there are things more evil than a jelly donut. (In
fact, in moderation, as a once-in-a-while treat, I see no evil in
donuts at all.) The point here, though, is the internal struggle.
The *continent* person struggles within himself against powerful desires, and prevails. The truly *temperate* person, on the contrary, has
trained himself to the point that he no longer feels the pull of
strong and vehement desires. The perfectly temperate man may
appreciate the pleasant qualities of a nice jelly donut, a pint of ale,
or a beautiful woman, without experiencing a strong inward compulsion to have them when he shouldn't.

However, continence can be a stepping-stone along the road to true temperance. The habitual practice of continence, saying no to our desires through repeated effortful acts, develops within us the talent of temperance, which, when perfected, eliminates the internal struggle altogether. Recall again St. Augustine's reference to temperance and integrity, or internal unity — in this case, a harmony between the appetites and the intellect.

When a man thinks of *modesty* in relation to temperance, perhaps women's clothing may first come to mind. It does not take much to draw the intemperate man (and few of us indeed, would claim perfection here) to lustful thoughts, and we live in the day of low-cut tops and low-rise bottoms, gym shorts with words emblazoned across the back, skin-tight jeans and skin-exposing swimwear leaving oh, so little to the male imagination.

I recall reading in my youth one of the unfortunate nineteenth-century philosopher Nietzsche's pining aphorisms, warning of girls with "a well-turned ankle." Today's fashions reveal so much more than ankles! St. Thomas does address modesty in apparel, and he recommends that clothing be fitting with the customs of one's society (the word *modesty* deriving from the word *mode*, or "the ordinary"), with one's role or station, with nature, and with humility. One's everyday attire should not be ostentatious either in its elegance or in its exaggerated plainness or simplicity (which may portray a spiritual pride). St. Thomas also notes, quite wisely and lovingly, that a married woman may do well to dress and adorn herself in a manner pleasing to her husband.

Modesty is about more than dress codes, however. St. Thomas also describes a modesty "consisting in the outward movement of the body." His exposition is full of delightful insights into human behavior (and its perfection). Also quite prescient, predating by sixteen centuries the modern observations of Adlerian psychology about the coherence of a person's "style of life" revealing itself in all manners of behavior, St. Ambrose wrote (echoing Sirach 19:29-30) that "the attire of the body, and the laughter of the teeth, and the gait of the man, show what he is." Further, "the habit of mind is seen in the gesture of the body," and "the body's movement is the index of the soul." Who we are shows in our facial expression, in our gait, and in our gestures. (Do you recall the bearing and the speech of the magnanimous man?) St. Augustine advises us "in all our movements, let nothing be done to offend the eye of another, but only that which is becoming to the holiness of your state" (ST, II-II, Q. 168, art. 1).

Do Curious Minds Want to
Know What's Worth Knowing?

In considering temperance, St. Thomas also provides a fascinating contrast between the related virtue of studiousness and its contrary vice of curiosity. *Studiousness* moderates the human desire to know — for there is much in this world that is not worth knowing, that feeds our baser desires and diverts us from higher things. The vice of *curiosity* is the desire to know and pry into things that we should leave alone. It creates and then feeds upon boredom and inattentiveness. Just look at that guy with the television remote-control, clicking away again and again and again. (Hey, that's not *you*, is it?) Studiousness, on the other hand, is the virtue whereby we seek out not fleeting entertainments, but lasting wisdom.

God's Grace: The Only True Guide to Temperance

St. Thomas, echoing the words of Psalms and Proverbs, tells us that of the gifts of the Holy Spirit, fear of the Lord most directly relates to the virtue of temperance, since it steers us away from the lusts of the flesh. Temperance is not an easy virtue. We can build the natural virtue of temperance through our repeated daily efforts, hoping that continence wins out over incontinence along the way. But true and perfect temperance can come only as a gift from God, when we "do not dwell on singulars," but rather, dwell on the source of all being, him from whom all "singulars" flow.

Blessed Are the Temperate

Every last blessed one of these talents, complete with its virtues, parts, and gifts, serves the ultimate goal of our ultimate happiness (that is, "beatitude") by bringing us closer to God. So which of the Beatitudes from Jesus' Sermon on the Mount most directly attests to the merits and rewards of temperance? Since temperance reins in our passion for excessive fleshly, earthly, or sensible goods, *poverty of spirit* is a beatitude of temperance.

God gave the noble philosopher Socrates a beautiful and simple poverty of spirit that Christians would do well to emulate. Once, while enjoying a stroll through the thriving *agora* (marketplace) of Athens, he exclaimed with excitement (I paraphrase), "Behold all these wonderful things I don't need!" (Would that we could do the same while meandering through the mall!)

Sixteen hundred years later, while walking along the streets of Paris, a wealthy man insisted on buying St. Thomas Aquinas a magnificent gift. Although reluctant at first, this most temperate of saints consented. As they passed a street lined with peddlers selling birds in cages, Thomas indicated his request. The rich man bought them all; the Angelic Doctor set them all free!

"Blessed are the meek." The natural virtue of *meekness* is a potential part of temperance that moderates or controls the exercise of our passions — in this case, anger. Those who take on the

meekness of Christ will temper their anger at their earthly brothers who might do them harm, and ironically, they "shall inherit the earth."

Finally, *purity of heart* is the beatitude bearing most directly on temperance's greatest challenge. Purity of heart raises our focus from selfish satisfactions of the flesh and the world toward the spiritual satisfactions that come from God. Happiness is fulfilled desire, while unhappiness is a sense of deprivation. When those with God's temperance, the pure of heart, behold something or someone of great beauty and allure, their hearts respond to God not, "Give me!" but "Thank you!"

PROFILES IN TALENT #7

St. Thomas the Temperate (c. 1225-1274)

Two of the greatest Doctors of the Church are sometimes referenced to illustrate opposite ends of the human continuum with regard to the powers of the stirrings of the flesh. St. Augustine famously prayed to God for chastity — "but not quite yet." His early adult life was spent reveling in the sins of the flesh. St. Thomas, on the other hand, was said to have been given a girdle of chastity as a young man, after chasing away with a firebrand a prostitute his brothers dispatched to sway him from his devotion to his religious order. Still, we are also told that St. Thomas was a very large man, raising the suspicion of intemperance in the food department. Stories are told of tables with their fronts cut away in a semicircle, so the portly saint would have room to sit and eat.

When it comes to the power of our concupiscible appetites for food and sex, there are substantial inborn individual differences. Still, it is the rarest of souls who is not prone to some extent to internal struggles between the appetites, the intellect, and the will. Perhaps the key to St. Thomas's success in the mastery of lust was his capacity to ignore the singulars, so immersed was he in the lofty things of God. And indeed, one singular he seems rarely to have noticed was himself. One finds, for example, very few self-references in his writings. One might suspect St. Thomas to be a man of pure reason, but simply read his poems and prayers, and you'll see his passions were indeed most powerful and moving, although they moved him closer to God.

Chapter 6

Justifying Justice

"It is justice that renders to each one what is his,
and claims not another's property; it disregards its
own profit in order to preserve the common equity."
St. Ambrose

"Justice is the most resplendent of the virtues,
and gives a man a good name."
Cicero

"The most excellent of the virtues would seem
to be justice, and more glorious than
either the evening or the morning star."
Aristotle

"When magnanimity is added to justice,
it increases the latter's goodness; and yet
without justice it would not even be a virtue."
St. Thomas Aquinas

Justice is like the moral talents of fortitude and temperance in that it perfects a power of the human appetites. Fortitude regulates the *irascible* appetite, temperance the *concupiscible* appetite, and justice, the *intellectual* appetite, known simply as the *will*.

Justice is unlike fortitude and temperance, however, in that its focus is not on oneself, but on others. Fortitude and temperance look inward, and rightly so, helping us to guide and control ourselves to seek the true good. (Indirectly, of course, they are certainly a boon to our neighbor as well. All persons do well to associate with the temperate and the brave.) But justice reaches out directly to our neighbor, reining in our self-interest.

St. Ambrose tells us that justice is about rendering to each person his *rightful due*. But just what is each person's due? What do we owe our neighbor? Would the Catholic theologian answer this question differently from the pagan philosopher? Are there some who have special claims upon our talents of justice? What specific kinds of actions would justice bid us do (and not do)? How can we build the talent of justice within our souls? These are but a few of the questions we'll try to give their rightful due in the pages ahead.

Putting the *Jus* in Justice

St. Thomas tells us that the word *justice* derives from the Latin word *jus* (or *ius*), which means "right." So what rights can our neighbors claim from us? Well, Americans know about "inalienable rights endowed in us by our Creator," and of "life, liberty, and the pursuit of happiness" that are expressed in our Declaration of Independence. The very concept of "inalienable rights," so dear to our Founding Fathers, owes much to the theory of law — natural law, manmade law, and eternal law — developed in the writings of none other than St. Thomas Aquinas. Indeed, we will see in our Profile in Talent at the end of this chapter that one of the greatest modern American champions of social justice appealed directly to the authority of St. Thomas in his arguments. The virtue of justice is also prescribed in every one of the Ten Commandments. When we worship only the true God, do not use his name in vain, and honor him on the Lord's Day, we render what is due to our Maker. When we honor our parents and abstain from killing, adultery, stealing, false witness, and coveting our neighbor's wife and goods, we render due rights to others.

Justice operates on two fundamental principles; its integral parts are "Do good" and "Do not do evil." The justice of the philosophers, or at least the justice of the law courts, focuses primarily on the second principle. We are not to deprive others of their rights, or we must pay the penalty of the law. But there is also a positive side to justice, which was pronounced most fully by Jesus Christ himself when he gave to us the summary of all the commandments: to love God with all our hearts and our neighbors as ourselves. For the follower of Christ, then, justice and the love that is charity become closely intertwined, as we seek not only not to hurt our brother, but to help him.

Putting the *Us* in Justice

Justice is a vast topic, one to which I truly cannot do justice here. St. Thomas addresses all varieties of law and justice: the laws of the courtroom, of the nation, between nations, and the eternal Law of God. Go to the *Summa Theologica* if you would care to be awed by all that justice entails. For our purposes, I am going to focus on *the personal habit of justice as a talent* that we may unearth and build within us. So let's begin by remembering that the natural cardinal virtues that underlie the talents of living are indeed *habits*. It might sound a little odd to think of justice as a habit, but if we are to build the talent of justice within our own souls, it should come to sound quite straightforward and familiar. You might say we need to make a habit of thinking of it that way.

Aristotle has noted that "justice is a habit whereby a man renders to each one his due by a constant and perpetual will," and further, "justice is a habit whereby a man is said to be capable of doing just actions in according with his choice" (*ST*, II-II, Q. 58, art. 1). Please note well the roles of habit, choice, will, and action. The capacity to be just to others must be built within ourselves through our habitual actions, day after day, through the training of our wills always to do what is right by our fellowman. Although it may not be easy, recall that, when perfected, the talent of justice is "more glorious than either the evening or the morning star."

THE PARTS OF JUSTICE

Integral parts	Subjective parts	Annexed parts	
Doing good	Commutative justice	Religion	Piety
Avoiding evil	Distributive justice	Observance	Gratitude
		Vengeance	Truth
		Friendliness	Liberality
			Epikeia

Justice deals with a myriad of complex legal and personal issues, but St. Thomas breaks them down most fundamentally to two basic types or subjects: *commutative justice*, which deals with the private matters of individuals dealing with one another, and *distributive justice*, which deals with matters of entire communities or states.

St. Thomas lists six potential virtues of justice that he derived from the writings of Cicero. These are religion, piety, observance, gratitude, vengeance (perhaps surprisingly), and truth. St. Thomas also writes about three other related virtues: friendliness, liberality, and something called *epikea*, which I won't be addressing here.[6] Friendship and friendliness will be covered in the chapter on charity, and liberality has already been mentioned in the context of magnificence. For now, the time is just right to see how we can apply what is just and right in our own daily lives and personal behaviors. Let's go, then, to the virtues annexed to justice.

It's Just Religion

Am I (and St. Thomas) saying that the virtue of religion is inferior or less important than the virtue of justice, since being only a potential part, it "falls short" of the full definition of justice? Good question. Let's hear St. Thomas on this one: "The precepts pertaining to religion are given precedence (Exod. 20) as being of greatest importance . . . Therefore religion is the chief of the moral virtues" (*ST*, II-II, Q. 81, art. 6). He is saying that the first three of the Ten Commandments are directed to giving God his due, and these are the most important. But religion nonetheless falls short of the full definition of justice because it entails giving another his rightful due *in equal measure*. Because of God's absolute greatness and generosity, *we can never give back to him in equal measure what he has given to us*. But this does not prevent the virtue

---

[6] *Epikea*, or equity, an intriguing virtue discussed by Aristotle, applies more specifically to legal justice than to personal justice. Please go to Thomas, (*ST*, II-II, Q. 120) if you'd like to learn more.

of religion (the habit of paying reverence to God) from being the greatest of all moral virtues. Let's dig in, then, and see what the virtue of *religion* is all about.

St. Isidore says that religion derives from the Latin word *relegit*, "to read again," whereas St. Augustine notes religion's relation to the Latin word *religare*, "to bind together." In practicing the virtue of religion, we do read again and again the Scriptures and ponder again and again divine truths. And the acts of religion confirm our "bond" with God. St. Thomas points out how both etymological senses of *religion* are especially apparent in the lives of religious men and women who are formally consecrated to God.

Let's remember that "a virtue is that which makes its possessor good, and his acts good likewise" (*ST*, II-II, Q. 81, art. 3). The virtue of religion, then, entails both *interior* and *exterior* acts. It perfects our wills by directing them to God, but it *begins* through the operations of our *intellects*, as we ponder God's greatness, and it *ends* in outward *actions: directly* in our acts of worship to God, and *indirectly* in the good deeds we perform for our neighbors, as God would have us do.

Interior acts of religion include devotion and prayer. *Devotion* implies that we have "vowed" ourselves to God and dedicated our heart to live for him. St. Thomas makes a very interesting point about how devotion ties into the talent of science, noting that sometimes those with great intent on acquiring and using scientific knowledge become overconfident in their powers and neglect God. However, "if a man perfectly submits to God his science or any other perfection, by the very fact his devotion is increased" (*ST*, II-II, Q. 81, art. 3).[7]

---

[7] Shortly before the dawn of the scientific marvels of the twentieth century (and shortly after the growing popularity of

Prayer is the other essential interior act of religion. And believe me, if your concept of prayer is a little vague or fuzzy, it won't be any more if you ever open up the *Summa Theologica* itself and ponder the seventeen articles the Angelic Doctor devotes to the subject. You will learn, for example, whether we should pray only directly to God, whether we should ask for specific things (and if so, if these include temporal or worldly things), why we should pray for others and for our enemies, why the seven petitions of the Lord's Prayer are "perfect," whether prayer is proper for a "rational being" (listen up, modern scientists/armchair critics of religion!), whether we should pray out loud, whether we must pay attention while we pray (not always!), whether God hears the prayers of sinners, and why the proper parts of prayer are supplications, prayers, intercessions, and thanksgivings.

Whew! There's quite a science to prayer, you see, and the Angelic Doctor is the master scientist. As usual, part of the reason St. Thomas knew so much was that he studied so extensively the great Fathers before him. For example, he quotes the great Eastern Doctor St. John Chrysostom, who noted that prayer for ourselves comes from *necessity*, whereas prayer for others from *fraternal* (brotherly) *charity*; and "the prayer that comes from fraternal charity is sweeter to God than that which comes out of necessity." Or another: St. Isidore pointed out quite wisely, "We say 'Our Father' and not 'My Father,' 'Give us' and not 'Give me.' "

the writings of Darwin), Pope Leo XIII wrote in his encyclical *Aeterni Patris* that for those who claimed "reason alone as their teacher and guide," there is no greater "cure for their unbelief" than the writings of the Scholastic Fathers. As for me, these great "doctors" did indeed prescribe just the medicine that I needed to cure my own unbelief and restore the desire to rebuild the virtue of religion in my soul!

As for the external acts of religion, St. Thomas addresses in depth a variety of actions, including adoration, sacrifice, oblations and firstfruits, tithes, oaths, and vows. Alas, space precludes further analysis here. (I'll never make it to the other parts of justice, let alone the remaining talents.) Go to Thomas and his *Summa*, and he will show you many other ways to go to God!

Heroic Piety

I've always had a tendency to conflate the virtues of *piety* and *religion*. Mention a pious person, and I'll think of someone who's religious. This is often pretty accurate. Indeed, God would certainly have us be pious, but there is also a more specific sense of the word.

When the ancient poet Virgil penned the *Aeneid*, his glorious epic tale extending Homer's *Iliad* from the ashes of Troy to the founding of Rome, his great hero Aeneas was often called "the pious." Early in the narrative we see Aeneas carrying his aged father Anchises upon his shoulders, guiding him to safety through the burning streets of Troy. Anchises did not want to leave at first, outraged at the sight of the burning citadel and desiring to defend his home against the victorious approaching Greeks. Aeneas, despite his own desires and his wife's pleading, prepared to don his armor to defend his father (and his fatherland) to the end.

Then a sign from the gods convinced Anchises that his family had a future in another land, and he became willing to flee. At this point, the pious Aeneas bent down upon his knee, spread a lion's pelt across his broad back, placed his aged father upon his sturdy shoulders, took his young son by the hand, and began the perilous journey that would eventually lead him, his family, and his friends to the founding of Rome.

There is an example of our particular meaning of the virtue of *pietas*, or piety: having a sense of special duty, not only to God, but to our parents and to our country. Notice how Aeneas donned the lion's skin — a symbol of heroic manhood both to the Jews, through Samson, and to the Greeks, through Hercules. Piously honoring one's parents in trying circumstances is no business for the fainthearted, and might well call forth the mighty virtue of fortitude to its aid.

"Honor your father and your mother." The fourth commandment directs us to piety. Are your parents still here on earth? Is there any small thing you can do today to serve them? Maybe they're a thousand miles away, but they have phones or email, don't they?

One of the most cherished simple after-work rituals of my early adult years was to call my mom, phone crooked in neck, while I caught up with the morning dishes, or helped my young wife get a head start on supper. I also fondly remember one Aeneas-like moment in my life. Mom had undergone some very rough times. She was debilitated from a near-death experience after heart-valve surgery and faced with returning from the hospital to a third-floor apartment (without an elevator) where she lived with my sister. I had the pious honor of carrying her up those flights, and the reward of her grateful smile.

If, like me, you are no longer able to pay respect to your parents in such simple ways, let's be mindful of the many avenues still open to us to honor their memories. We can pray for them, pray to them, and try to develop in ourselves the talents we know they would want us to have.

Observance Observed

Have you ever seen the bumper sticker that reads "Question Authority"? I can appreciate the suggestion that we should use those intellectual souls of ours to think for ourselves, rather than blindly accepting whatever authorities tell us. We've all been blessed with the interior voice of conscience — a law inscribed in man's heart by God — "man's most secret inner core and his sanctuary," as well as "a judgment of reason" whereby we judge the morality of our actions (CCC, pars. 1776-1777).

While we are to obey the dictates of our conscience, we also need to see that our conscience has been well formed, that our reason and judgment have been informed with the wisdom of God. We need to be careful that we don't presume too much of our own unaided judgment on moral matters, though, becoming overly skeptical or cynical of the motivations of those who are "in authority."

This hypercriticality seems especially common in the realm of politics today, and to some extent, rightly so. Consider, for example, Catholic politicians who believe they can act in good conscience against the most fundamental teachings of the Magisterium (not to mention the Fifth Commandment) on the basic right to human life. Should the will of the majority (let alone a vocal minority) and the complicated practical concerns of politics trump moral absolutes in an elected official's decisions on issues affecting the lives of thousands or millions? This question is not new.

Some have said we have many *politicians*, but few *statesmen* anymore. We might hesitate even to call them politicians. Listen to this one: "But the majority of those engaged in politics are not correctly designated as 'politicians,' for they are not truly political, since the political man is one who purposely chooses noble actions for their own sake, whereas the majority embrace that mode of life for the sake of money and gain." Sound a little familiar? Well, that statement did not come from commentary from the last election. It came over 2,300 years ago from Aristotle in his *Eudemian Ethics*.

Unearthing Your Ten Talents

So what does this have to do with *observance*? St. Thomas says that according to Cicero, "it is by observance that we pay worship and honor to those who excel in some way in honor" (*ST*, II-II, Q. 102, art. 2). We know that our parents exceed us in honor, and all the more so does God. As we've just seen, that's where the virtues of piety and religion come in. But there are many others who excel us in honor, in terms of their own excellence, or by virtue of some position of authority they have been granted by their efforts and God's graces. Examples that St. Thomas provides include governing officials, commanding officers in the military, and teachers. We could also include our bosses at work or clergy at church. And more broadly speaking, Thomas argues that in some ways, we all owe observance to *each other*. Let's spell this out.

There are two main parts to the virtue of observance, and these are *dulia* and *obedience*. *Dulia* means honor or respect to a person's excellence. To build the talent of justice, we need to show honor where honor is due. Aristotle tells us that honor is the proper reward of virtue, and we're commanded by Christ himself that we are not to hide our lights under a bushel basket (Matt. 5:15), but to let them shine forth among men (Matt. 5:15). St. Thomas tells us that *dulia* is principally shown through word and deeds, and by gestures such as bowing or saluting. I happen to live in a city that shows great *dulia* honoring the excellence of its favorite son, a man of great justice, Abraham Lincoln. His light truly shined forth among men, and due *dulia* is shown him by a plethora of statues, buildings, streets, books, shops, and assorted memorabilia bearing his image or his story.

But every person in every town can also demonstrate *dulia* every day on a smaller, but no less important scale. St. Thomas states explicitly that *in every other person we can find some quality or talent in which his excellence exceeds our own*. Hence, we all owe some measure of the respect and honor of *dulia* to one another. St. Paul has told us as much: "In humility count others better than your-selves. Let each of you look not only to his own interests, but to the interests of others" (Phil. 2:3-4).

Bending our will to the interests of others leads us to the sec-ond part of observance, that of *obedience*. We need to show obedi-ence to God, and one way we do this is in our obedience to the rightful authority of those placed over us, for it ultimately comes from God. In the words of St. Gregory the Great, by obeying those in authority over us, we "slay our own will" in the spirit of charity. Indeed, charity, that greatest of talents, cannot exist without obe-dience. "He who says, 'I know him' but disobeys his command-ments is a liar, and the truth is not in him; but whoever keeps his word, in him truly love for God is perfected" (1 John 2:4-5). So, short of those rare situations in which a well-formed conscience cannot obey an external authority, to display both justice and charity, sometimes we must subdue our own wills and question *our own* authority, when obedience is due to an individual placed above us with a higher excellence or position than our own.

Thanks for the Gratitude

The individual with the talent for justice seeks to repay debts: debts to God (although these can never be repaid in full) through the virtue of *religion*, debts to parents and country through *piety*, debts to those excelling in dignity through *observance*, and also debts to benefactors, to those who grant particular and private fa-vors or benefits, through the virtue of *gratiarum actio* — thankful-ness or gratitude. Cicero rightly placed *gratitude* as one of the virtues annexed to justice, but it was another ancient Roman phi-losopher, Lucius Anneas Seneca (4 B.C.-A.D. 65), who literally wrote the book on gratitude (*De Beneficiis* — "On Benefits"). When analyzing this virtue, St. Thomas shares liberally from Seneca's silver-tongued words of counsel. I can barely do it justice here, but I'll try to show a little gratitude for what these great men have shared on this subject by introducing you to some highlights and praying that you will seek out more, both in the *Summa* and in the writings of Seneca.

"Give thanks in all circumstances," counsels St. Paul (1 Thess. 5:18). Let us consider the ways to give these thanks, beginning with "in all circumstances." Are you ever tempted to disregard a favor from someone? "Well, she was just nice because she wanted something." "His wife told him he should do it." "He didn't really want to do it for me, but he felt pressure from his boss, his coworkers, or friends." "He just gave them to me because he didn't want them himself. Everybody knows he can't stand black jelly beans!" "He gave me the money. So what? He's rich, and it was nothing to him." "Sure he put in a good word to get me that promotion, but he just wanted to show his clout." (Again I'm reminded of Aristotle's comment on virtue and how there are so many ways to *miss* the bull's-eye.)

Let's hear Seneca on this one: "It is the height of malevolence to refuse to recognize a kindness, unless the giver has been the loser thereby." How petty it is to feel no gratitude to our benefactor unless we should first decide that his motives were pure, or that he had suffered in some way through his gift to us! St. Thomas chimes in with his trademark depth of wisdom and kindness: "It is the mark of a happy disposition to see good rather than evil. Wherefore, if someone has conferred a favor not as he ought have conferred it, the recipient should not for that reason withhold his thanks."

How, then, do we show our gratitude to our benefactors in all circumstances? Seneca says, "Do you wish to repay a favor? Receive it graciously." Even if we are benefitted by someone so rich or power-ful that we can never repay him in kind, we can still repay by our attitude, our facial expression, our words, and our deeds, or as Seneca notes with "good advice, frequent fellowship, affable and pleasant conversation without flattery." Further, the grateful "out-pourings of one's heart" should be heard, not only within the benefactor's earshot, but within the hearing of others, repaying the benefactor with well-earned honor — which is virtue's right-ful reward. The benefactor who receives some well-earned esteem might then be all the more inspired to seek new ways to continue to benefit others.

When benefits are to be repaid, we should do so promptly and gladly, but we should not be in such a hurry to repay that we incon-venience the giver, or make him feel we have been made uncom-fortable by the very favor he conferred. And what, then, is the height of ingratitude? It is not to fail to repay the favor, because we might not always be able to repay, although we would dearly like to. The height of ingratitude is to *forget* the favor or ignore the debt through negligence.

Surely we've all sinned through ingratitude at one time or an-other. When we are on the receiving end of ingratitude, however, we remember that Jesus told us to "lend, expecting nothing in re-turn" (Luke 6:35). Quite fittingly, St. Thomas advises us that "he that bestows a favor must not at once act the part of a punisher of ingratitude, but rather that of a kindly physician, by healing the ingratitude with repeated favors."

When Vengeance Is Just

Are you surprised to see vengeance listed as a virtue? Well, some sins are worse than ingratitude and do require a punishment. This is where the virtue of *vengeance* comes in. Cicero tells us that "by vengeance we resist force, or wrong, and in general, whatever is obscure [i.e., derogatory], either by self-defense or by avenging it." Vengeance is related to the "irascible appetite," whereby we achieve the "arduous good" by fighting evils and removing obstacles to the good. Its execution may call forth as well the virtue of fortitude. Vengeance as a virtue, then, is not vigilantism or lack of mercy, but rather, is the habit of punishing wrongdoing *within the realm of one's rightful authority*, and in the spirit of helping the wrongdoer, or at least protecting innocent victims. Vengeance must be exercised with great care, however; punishment must be delayed while one is angered, and those with the virtue of vengeance will be slow to take vengeance for wrongdoings they themselves receive.

The vice opposed to vengeance by way of excess is cruelty or brutality, while the vice of deficiency is being remiss in punishing when it is truly called for. Proverbs 13:24 mentions just this lack of virtuous vengeance: "He who spares the rod hates his son, but he who loves him is diligent to discipline him." And please note well the "loves" in that proverb, and recall again that for the Christian, justice and love should always be two sides of the same virtuous coin.

The Truth About Justice

We owe each other the truth. What we believe or know should correspond with what we say. To tell the truth is a good act. To develop within ourselves the habit of telling the truth, then, is a moral virtue. Truth's vice of deficiency arises when we hide what ought to be known, such as in refusing to admit or lying about a misdeed that we ought to confess. The vice of excess involves piping up with the truth when it is "out of season," unnecessary, or inappropriate. On a minor level, this applies to those statements that might provoke a sarcastic "thanks for sharing that" type of remark. On a more serious level, it applies to telling truths that could belittle, demoralize, or be in some way unnecessarily hurtful to another.

"Thou shall not bear false witness against thy neighbor," states the Eighth Commandment. The sundry vices (of varying levels of seriousness) that oppose truth include false witness in a formal legal setting, lying in general, dissimulation (or false pretense), hypocrisy, as well as exaggeration and boasting about virtues or accomplishments that are not true. As St. Thomas catalogues these vices, I'm reminded yet again of Aristotle's comment on the many ways the arrow can miss the bull's-eye.

But here's a surefire way to hit the target of truth all your life, from him who is "the way, and the truth, and the life" (John 14:6). I'll bet you've heard it. It goes, "Whatsoever you wish that men would do to you, do so to them" (Matt. 6:12). Do you enjoy being lied to? Our intellectual souls are designed to seek truth, and in situations where we cannot ascertain it directly ourselves, but must rely on the testimony of others, we certainly all wish that those others are truly reliable.

Justice and the Great-Souled Man

We can gather from St. Thomas's quotation at this chapter's start that when loftiness of thought and greatness of soul are superadded to the virtues of justice, justice itself is enhanced and ennobled. (Pretty impressive on magnanimity's part, eh?) But note well that without justice, magnanimity is no virtue at all. We need look back only to the early and mid-twentieth century to find real historical figures with the most grandiose projects and goals for entire peoples and continents. They proposed to erect noble utopias to the glory of man, yet, lacking respect for the basic God-given rights of every human life, Hitler, Stalin, and their brothers in spirit who paraded across history brought hells, not heavens, to earth.

Consider this in light of one absolutely essential aspect of magnanimity. The great-souled individual never considers himself *the* great-souled individual. He never fails to acknowledge the greatness of soul that God has also bestowed upon *all human persons*, regardless of race, politics, sex, age, ability, disability, or any particular characteristics. Indeed, the great in soul expend their power to protect and uplift, and never to belittle or squelch the potential for greatness in others. St. Thomas was so right when he told us that without justice, magnanimity would be no virtue at all.

Blessed Are the Spirit's Gifts of Justice

The talent of justice implies more than merely the natural virtue of justice and its parts. When justice is not only directed to God as in religion, but directly inspired, infused, and rewarded by God, we see it expressed in the gifts, the Beatitudes, in the fruits of the Holy Spirit, and in the sacraments of the Catholic Church.

The gift of the Holy Spirit connected to justice is the gift of *piety*. We saw how the natural virtue of piety directs our reason in honoring our parents. Through the gift of piety, the Holy Spirit directs us in honoring *God as our Father*. Beatitudes relating directly to justice include the bearing of persecution (recall how vengeance is more tolerant of wrongdoings toward oneself), mercifulness (justice is more than "an eye for an eye and a tooth for a tooth"), and peacemaking (true peace and harmony both between and within individuals, being closely aligned as well with the talents of *wisdom* as we have seen, and of *charity*, yet to come).

Of the fruits of the Holy Spirit, St. Thomas tells us the one bearing most directly on justice is that of *kindness*. (Kindness itself is a virtue of such importance that we'll address it later in the chapters on charity and on practical application of the virtues.) Lastly, when early Church Fathers paired virtues to the most closely related sacraments, the sacrament of Reconciliation was paired with justice, since in this sacrament God gives us his mercy when we show contrition for failing to give him and our neighbors their rightful due.

The Sacrament *and Virtue* of Penance

This sacrament pertaining most directly to justice is also commonly known as Confession or Penance. With his usual perceptiveness and profundity, St. Thomas also notes that there is a sense in which *penance is itself a virtue*, complete with integral parts, and that the *sacrament of Penance* works through God's grace to *restore other virtues*. The integral parts of the *virtue* of penance that Thomas explains in Part III of the *Summa Theologica* are the same three parts you will find in paragraphs 1451 through 1460 in the *Catechism of the Catholic Church* on the sacrament of Reconciliation — namely, *contrition, confession of sins,* and *satisfaction*. When we are truly penitent, we appeal to God's justice and mercy by *feeling sorrow* within our hearts for our sins, by *outwardly admitting* them to the priest, and by *making amends by the actions* prescribed by the confessor, be they prayers, reflections, good deeds, or specific acts of reparation.

To truly unearth the talent of justice, then, we must dig deep within our conscience to unearth the virtue of penance, and allow God to heal and build us through the grace of his sacrament of Penance as well.

PROFILES IN TALENT #8

A Talent for Justice:
Dr. Martin Luther King, Jr. (1929-1968)

Today is January 21, and as a government employee, I am off work today to celebrate the birthday of Dr. Martin Luther King, Jr. I'm going to do so by praising one of his exceedingly important talents: an undying passion for justice.

Justice, St. Thomas told us, means "giving to each his rightful due." Surely, most of us today are aware that in the 1950s and 1960s African-Americans in the United States were not being given some of the rights that were rightfully theirs. Surely, you know how Dr. King, a Baptist minister and a champion for social justice, fought tirelessly against injustice and paid the price with his own life. But are you aware of the spiritual, intellectual, moral, and legal connection between Dr. King and St. Thomas Aquinas?

In his famous "Letter from a Birmingham Jail," written on Easter weekend of 1963, while he was confined for protesting against segregation without a legal permit, Dr. King wrote, "To put it in the terms of St. Thomas Aquinas: An unjust law is a human law that is not rooted in eternal law and natural law. Any law that uplifts human personality is just. Any law that degrades human personality is unjust."

Dr. King looked to the day when we would be judged, not by the color of our skin, but by the content of our character. We would do well to improve the content of our characters by emulating the talent for justice that good Dr. King so justly displayed.

Chapter 7

Practicing Prudence

*"Prudence has the nature of virtue not only as the
other intellectual virtues have it but also as the moral
virtues have it, among which virtues it is enumerated."*
St. Thomas Aquinas

"Prudence is right reason applied to action."
St. Thomas Aquinas

Prudence, or practical wisdom, has a special nature that places it at the head of the cardinal virtues. The *Catechism of the Catholic Church* refers to prudence as the *auriga virtutum*, or "charioteer of the virtues" (par. 1806) because of its guiding function. Prudence is "right reason applied to action." It lives at the intersection of the realms of the true and the good, the intellect and the will, thought and action, the universal and the singular, intellectual and moral virtue. Prudence seeks out the best and most moral means for achieving virtuous ends and directs us in their execution.

Have I studied long enough for this difficult examination, or is it time to call it quits and relax? (In other words, have I duly exercised my talent of *fortitude* in this situation?) Faced with this enormous box of donuts by the office coffee pot, is the act I am contemplating a *temperate* one? Should I respond in kind to that driver's gesture, or ignore it and go calmly on my way? In other words, how can I respond *justly* to his "road rage"? It is through the virtue of *prudence* that we arrive at the answers to such questions *and act upon them*.

Prudence, you see, decides what needs to be done, and gets it done. When exercising the talent of prudence, we *reflect* upon possible courses of action, *judge* which is best, and then *do it*.

Practical Wisdom Looks Back for the Future

When deciding which course of action is the best to take in a given situation, we must try to predict the outcome. We say to ourselves that our chosen plan is most likely to work, to bring about the desired end. There is always this futuristic or forward-looking aspect to prudence, which is why it was known in Latin as *providentia*, which means "to see before" or to have foresight. But there is so much more to the practical wisdom that is prudence. It is intermeshed with the present and past as much as with the future. Indeed, you'll see shortly that no less a brilliant and devout Doctor of the church than St. Albert the Great argued that the part of prudence that relates to the *past* is the most important of all. To show you what I mean, I think the most prudent course of action is for us to dig right into the integral parts of prudence.

THE PARTS OF PRUDENCE

Integral parts		Subjective parts	Annexed parts
Memory	Understanding	Governing self	Eubolia
Docility	Shrewdness	Governing others	Synesis
Reason	Foresight		Gnome
Caution	Circumspection		

Muse's Mother Meets Medieval Memory Masters

When we use the word *mnemonic* to describe systems for improving our memory powers, we are borrowing from the name of Mnemosyne, the ancient Greek goddess of memory. Mnemosyne carried the title of "Mother of the Muses." The story goes that with their father, Zeus, the mightiest of all the Olympian gods, she bore nine daughters, each presiding over a major human art or science. You see, those wise old Greeks realized that memory is of fundamental importance to human achievement in virtually any endeavor, and this is a lesson that did not escape two great Catholic theological Doctors and "medieval memory masters."

When St. Thomas addressed the virtue of prudence, he produced a state-of-the-art synthesis, employing and integrating
the best of the ideas of his philosophical predecessors, including
Cicero and Aristotle, and, characteristically for St. Thomas, perfecting them with insights from Scripture and the Church Fathers.
Personally, I've found his enumeration of the integral parts of prudence to be of immense importance and practical usefulness, as
my first book, *Memorize the Faith!* actually grew from the seed that
was St. Thomas's consideration of "Whether Memory Is a Part of
Prudence." Well, we know that St. Thomas's answer to that was a
resounding yes! Let's see why.

Thomas knew well that Cicero had identified the three parts of
prudence as *memory, understanding,* and *foresight,* because to perform wise actions producing good results in the future, we must act
in the present, guided by our understanding of the present situation and by the knowledge we have acquired through the past experiences we house in our memory. Thomas's teacher, St. Albert the
Great, had studied memory in depth: both the nature of human
memory and the techniques devised to improve it. He addressed
memory when discussing the virtue of prudence in his book *De
Bono* — "On the Good." Indeed, although foresight is sometimes
used synonymously with prudence, St. Albert argued that *memory*
is indeed *the most important part,* "because from past events we are
guided in the present and the future, and not from the converse"
(cited in Mary Carruthers, *The Book of Memory,* p. 275).

Practical wisdom is a product of knowledge and experience
that comes only with time to those who learn and retain life's
hard-won lessons. Sts. Albert and Thomas, accordingly, strongly
advocated training oneself in the specific techniques of "artificial
memory" practiced by the ancient Greeks and Romans, so as to be
able to retain and recall insights of profound ethical value — such

as lessons from Scripture and the Church Fathers. (The techniques themselves were the basis for *Memorize the Faith!*) Our task here is to become aware that if we are to build the talent of prudence within ourselves, we must also seek to unearth our powers of memory. Mnemosyne, then, is the mother not only of the muses, but also of the virtue of prudence.

The Particulars of Understanding

We need to get a bit nuanced here, in our understanding of understanding as a part of the virtue of prudence. In chapter 1, we saw understanding as the intellectual soul's *power* to "penetrate to the heart of things," to transcend the sense impressions of singular things to obtain their universal essence. We also saw understanding as the *intellectual virtue* that perfects that power by grasping self-evident universal principles. Here, though, we must also employ understanding in a fine-tuned, more *particular* sense. Prudence deals with practical, real-life situations, so the job of *understanding* as a part of prudence is twofold: we must understand universal ethical principles as perfected by the intellectual virtue of understanding, and we must understand how these principles should be applied to guide our own choices and actions in particular, specific, singular, real-world actions.

Let's proceed, then, with an actual real-world example calling upon the understanding of prudence in a big way. It is a situation that every single one of us faces in our lives, sometimes many times, *and which I, your author, am actually facing on the very day I am writing this.* It is a matter of vocation or career choice — specifically, whether to accept a promotion and/or position of greater responsibility and impact. Here is my dilemma: depending upon the personnel rules governing promotion within my government agency, I may receive a phone call within the next few days asking whether I will accept a new position that would move my responsibilities from supervising seven individuals' daily work to overseeing all the training activities of an office of several hundred.

Okay, so how am I going to employ the understanding of prudence here to make the right decision? I want my decision to be prudent — in accord with right reason and morally correct. Jumping back one integral part of prudence, I have been periodically tapping into my *memory*, including my own experience of previous similar career decisions. I have usually fared very well when choosing to advance, with the exception of one decision that I later found to be mistaken, leading me to a position that was a poor match for my skills, and from which I later removed myself. What lessons did I learn from both my positive and negative experiences in dealing with promotions and other major work decisions?

While I keep combing my memory intermittently, I am also trying to apply understanding. What kind of universal ethical principles apply here? The most general principle is to do good and avoid evil, so, of course, I want to make the choice that will do the most good for me, my office, and my family, and to avoid possible harm to others, including my present and possible future employees. Many other related principles come into play here, of course. I will need to practice humility and examine my conscience to be sure the decision is not based on pride, on striving to be known and admired based on position, since my memory also reminds me that pride "goeth" before falls. On the other hand, I know we are also called to magnanimity and the pursuit of great and worthy goals. We are not to hide our lights under bushel baskets (Matt. 5:15) — and, as we know so well, neither are we to let our talents remain buried underground!

So, then, bearing in mind such principles as the imperative to do good, to avoid evil, and to make the most of my talents, I must move from the universal to the particular as I try to understand how this particular decision to accept or decline advancement will embody or conflict with these universal moral guidelines. Do I believe I can really do good things to start new people in this career and help the experienced job veterans to advance even further and to better serve the public? Do my own specific abilities and experience match well with this position? Will the welfare of my current employees be negatively impacted? The understanding of prudence requires that I consider the specifics and particulars, both of the new position and my own capacities, to ensure that my decision will be a good one — not just a financially good one, but a morally good one.

There is so much more to consider, and that's why there are six more parts to prudence! Let's carry on.

Docile Doctors Practice Prudence

Today, being "docile" may conjure up images of being passive, of just "going with the flow."[8] But *docility*, from the Latin *docere* ("to teach"), really means being capable of being taught, being capable of learning from others and from experience. It is a virtuous attitude of intellectual humility. Proverbs 3:5 tells us, "Do not rely

---

[8] It's a sad fact that many of the classic virtues and vices have become corrupted and have come to be known today only in their bare-boned forms. Consider as examples the unflattering connotations of prudence associated with being a "prude," the negative and limited connotations of temperance associated with abstinence from alcohol or kill-joy tendencies in general, or the equation of sloth with a general laziness, overlooking its spiritual component. Indeed, in some usage, *virtue* itself has been reduced to sexual purity alone. Fortunately for us, we have the talented Thomas to show us the virtues in their full-bodied excellence.

on your own insight," and St. Thomas expounds that "in matters of prudence, man stands in very great need of being taught by others, especially by old folk who have acquired a sane understanding of the ends in practical matters" (*ST*, II-II, Q. 49, art. 3).

Docility is especially necessary for prudent behavior in the young. Moving back to my own dilemma: if I accept a position in charge of training, I will certainly hope that the new recruits are docile and trainable! But in making this decision (and in performing the new job, if that is the outcome) the trainer himself must remain trainable! How can I practice docility in making this decision? Well, one thing I can do is seek information from those already involved in training, from my new potential employees doing the first-line training, and from the administrators to whom I would answer.

St. Thomas makes clear that the docility of prudence is not only for the young: "Even the learned should be docile in some respects, since no man is altogether self-sufficient in matters of prudence" (*ST*, II-II, Q. 49, art. 3). Indeed, his continual references to his predecessors, and his peerless grasp of the subtleties of their messages, demonstrate the supreme docility that the greatest of the doctors, St. Thomas Aquinas himself, possessed. (And that's part of the reason I'm praying for the Angelic Doctor's intercession!)

The Untaming of Shrewdness

The fourth part that contributes to the whole that is prudence was known in the Latin as *sollertia* — a quick cleverness, or *shrewdness*. Ever the logician, Aristotle noted that "shrewdness consists in easily finding the middle term for demonstrations" (cited in *ST*, II-II, Q. 49. art. 4).

In case that description failed to produce an "aha" regarding shrewdness, let me add that "the middle term for demonstrations" brings us back to the realm of understanding how practical actions relate to universal ethical principles. To make this understandable, I'm afraid I have no choice but to throw a little syllogism your way right now (praying that you will demonstrate the patience of fortitude with me).

Aristotle systematized one of logic's variations in the form of the *syllogism*, consisting of a *major premise*, a *minor premise* (i.e., "middle term"), and a conclusion.

An old schooldays classic example goes as follows:

All men are mortal (*major premise*).
Socrates is a man (*minor premise, or middle term*).
Therefore, Socrates is mortal (*conclusion*).

We'll look a little more closely at the reasoning involved in our very next section, but for now, please peruse that minor premise or middle term, in this case, "Socrates is a man." This is the particular instance of the universal rule. If I were shrewd enough, I might be able to grasp the "middle term" of my own dilemma in an instant flash of insight, as in:

Always do the good.
This new position is the good.
Therefore, take this new position.

Unfortunately, of course, this is a situation where I can't be so sure of that middle term. The syllogism could look like this:

Always do the good.
This new position is *not* the good.
Therefore, do *not* take this new position.

Sometimes shrewdness does come into play in career decisions. For other positions of similar rank that require special attention to computer systems or administrative details, I can instantly pick out the middle term and say "This new position is *not* the good" (for me). This is what St. Thomas calls the "easy and rapid discernment" that is shrewdness. As he tells us: "Just as docility consists in a man being well-disposed to acquire a right opinion from another man, so shrewdness is an apt disposition to acquire a right estimate by oneself" (*ST,* II-II, Q. 49. art. 4).

Many situations, however, are beyond the limits of shrewdness, even in the most prudent of individuals, and that's why we need all the parts, including docility! But even in those difficult decisions, once we have gathered all the facts and assembled all the parts, that "aha!" of shrewdness might still come into play later on. (I sure hope so!)

The Reasons for Reason's Role

The *reason* essential to prudence refers to our human capacity to follow chains of arguments and arrive at logical conclusions. We can see how its role has been hinted at already in all of its previously considered: *memory, understanding, docility,* and *shrewdness*. They are the capacities that help to provide the subject matter, cognitive capacity, and willingness to think things through carefully. The integral parts of reason specially address that process of thinking things through.

Now it is time for a slightly more detailed second look at the syllogism. Here we go again:

All men are mortal (*major premise*).
Socrates is a man (*minor premise, or middle term*).
Therefore, Socrates is mortal (*conclusion*).

The word *syllogism* derives from Greek words meaning "to reckon or reason together." It is a means of coming to logical conclusions based on general and particular information captured in *major* and *minor* propositions, or *premises*.

If the major and minor premises hold true, the conclusion must follow. This form, of course, holds true to all manner of contents (factual or otherwise), and can be expressed even in symbols; for example, "All A are B. C is A. Therefore, C is B."

Consider, for example, this variation: "All Catholics are Christians. Joe is a Catholic. Therefore, Joe is a Christian." This is a valid syllogism, meaning the conclusion must follow the premises. But suppose we substituted the syllogism, "All A are B. C is B. Therefore, C is A." Nope. Not valid. This would give us, "All Catholics are Christians. Joe is a Christian. Therefore, Joe is a Catholic." It would be nice if it were *true* that Catholics and Christians were one and the same, but the logical form of the syllogism itself does not compel the conclusion. Reading "All A are B" as if equivalent to "All B are A" is an error called "converting the terms" of the premises, which seems to account for many of the errors people make in deductive reasoning with syllogisms. (That's because A might be either the same as B, or only a part of it.)

Leaving logical reasoning errors aside for the moment, the most important thing to remember is that for a conclusion of a syllogism to tell us something true, *the premises it is based on must be true*. This is fundamental when we desire to use our reasoning abilities to guide us toward correct actions in the real world. Let's get back at it.

First, we can deduce *logically valid* conclusions that are nonetheless patently *false* in the real world; these arise when the content of our premises is not true. Second, syllogistic reasoning can be used not only for description of facts (the realm of what "is") but also in a proscriptive form (the realm of what "ought to be" — in fact, this is how it applies in the world of prudence). Consider this syllogism: "Superior men should rule the destinies of others. I am a superior man. Therefore, I should rule the destiny of others." Let's cast it in the form of, "All A are B" (all superior men are those who should rule over the destinies of others), "C is A" (I am a superior man), "therefore C is B" (I should rule over the destinies of others). This is a *logically valid* syllogism. Alas, it is of the type that might have appealed to the reason of Hitler.

The lesson here again is that if reasoning is to guide us to true ethical behavior, then the premises from which we reason must also be *true*. To her credit, one of the philosopher Ayn Rand's favorite sayings was "Check your premises!" (If only she had examined some of her own ethical premises in the light of the writings of Thomas Aquinas!)

Back now to prudence, and to my career decision! For goodness' sake, neither Aristotle nor St. Thomas, indeed, not even I, would suggest that I must sit down to work out some syllogisms in order to decide whether to take the new job. (Let me see now. Let A represent the good, C represent the new position — no, I'm not going there.) These are processes that go on *implicitly, covertly within our intellects*, as we weigh pros and cons, seeking a prudent decision.

In my particular example, let's stick with the very general major premise of "Do the good." If I then *understand*, aided either by *docility* or *shrewdness*, that the new job is good for me (indeed, a greater good than my current position), then my *reason* compels the prudent logical conclusion that I should accept it, if it is offered. Of course, my rational faculties will actually be grasping with multiple reasoning processes based on multiple principles, which we will address most specifically in our consideration of *circumspection*.

In Foresight, It Must be Right

I ask you now to use your *memory*, to recall that *foresight* is virtuously synonymous with prudence, and that St. Thomas did consider it to be an essential part. Prudence, remember, seeks to find virtuous *means* to virtuous ends. Prudence bears a special relation to foresight, because prudence deals with practical and contingent matters, things in the future that might or might not come to be. It is, of course, no longer in our power to alter the events of the past. Therefore, the prudent individual seeks to predict the likely future results of his present behaviors, guided by what he has learned in the past.

Foresight, then, implies another form of hypothetical "if-then" reasoning, representing our best attempts at predicting the future, based on what we know today. If I take this job, what is likely to follow? I want the best possible outcome for myself, my office, and my family, but is this new position really the proper means to that end? I've got to think ahead when forming a prudent decision. What are the potential consequences of my actions? How long do I plan on working before retiring? What impact is this likely to have on my other responsibilities outside of work? Might the greater demands decrease my reserve energy and capacities for other activities — such as writing? All these things and more must be considered as I pull from my memory while reasoning out my decision.

Look Up, Look Down, Look All Around

Circumspection derives from words meaning "to look all around," to take all the present circumstances into consideration when making a decision. For an example of this talent, allow me to recall a character from my book *Fit for Eternal Life*: the mightiest of Greek athletes, Milo of Croton. Suppose Milo were to seek a virtuous end — to glorify God by making the most of his bodily, athletic talents — and to achieve this end, he strives to make himself physically stronger. Now, legend has it that as a lad, Milo grew strong by regularly lifting a young calf as it gradually grew into a mature bull. As the bull grew bigger and stronger, so, too, grew mighty Milo! So let's suppose that Milo, seeking to achieve his end through prudent means, asks the simple, practical question: "Do I lift my calf *today?*"

Milo searches his memory for the principles of weightlifting and of rest; he recalls and *understands* the simple principles of progressive resistance strength training; and he hearkens back with *docility* to the counsels of the trainers of his youth, although now he relies mostly on the *shrewdness* in training matters that has come with time and experience. He sets his *reason* to work on the question, bearing in mind with *foresight* the likely results. Typically, after a round of lifting his bull, he comes back later all the stronger. But let's suppose that one day Milo prudently decides that rather than hoisting his prize bull, he's going to spend the day collecting seashells on the shores of the Mediterranean.

Why? Well, perhaps Milo has decided, through the process of *circumspection*, to exercise his mind rather than his muscles today. In all sorts of practical, real-world situations, circumstances will play a role in the practical decisions we make. Perhaps, in Milo's case, the special circumstance is that he tweaked or strained his biceps while wrestling the day before. Therefore, he realizes that although calf-lifting is needed to build his strength, if he's recovering from an injury it can also cause harm and make him weaker.

St. Thomas provides a short, sweet, ethical example of the application of circumspection. Suppose, he says, you desire to show someone some sign of love, "to be a fitting way to arouse love in his heart, yet if pride or suspicion of flattery arise in his heart, it will no longer be a means to a suitable end" (*ST*, II-II, Q. 49. art. 7). In this case, perhaps you hold back on your show of approval or affection, because you realize that with this particular individual, or in light of these particular circumstances (perhaps he or she has just done something unworthy of praise), an undesired result will likely follow.

Prudence, remember, when faced with the practical and real-world situations of our daily lives, cannot operate entirely like a mathematical formula with a definitive answer or like a purely logical syllogism, with all the premises laid out for us. Prudence requires that we use our intellectual faculties to guide us as well as possible, considering all the surrounding circumstances, both seen and unseen. Circumspection, then, will prompt us to try to see and consider those concrete circumstances that can make all the difference.

But, hey, wait a minute. What about me? Moving back again to my own real-time, real-life job decision, I must try to factor in all the various circumstances and variables. Very important considerations for me include my current commitments and deadlines for writing, as well as my prospects for being able to continue to write in the future. I must consider how this could be impacted by the outside circumstances, and also by my personal characteristics and my unique abilities. I can draw upon my moral and intellectual models and heroes, especially those who may have had similar temperaments and abilities (although in an immeasurably greater magnitude).

St. Thomas, for example, showed no interest in repeated opportunities and offerings of "promotions" along the lines of becoming an abbot or a bishop, because he wanted to dedicate himself to his study, writing, and teaching. On the other hand, Thomas's own teacher, St. Albert the Great, also became the great bishop of Ratisbon. Although I'll never be proffered such a glorious position, his example is also worthy of consideration as I use circumspection to weigh all possible factors in order to reach a prudent decision.

Caution: Slippery Decision Ahead

Somewhere it has been said that fools jump in where angels fear to tread. Earlier we contrasted foolishness with wisdom, and rashness with fortitude, but when it comes to practical matters calling forth wisdom, fortitude, or any other virtue, *caution*, too, falls within prudence's domain. Caution is the eighth and final integral part of prudence.

St. Paul advises, "Look carefully [*cautiously* in St. Thomas's translation], then, how you walk, not as unwise men, but as wise" (Eph. 5:15). Consider again that prudence deals with practical, real-world issues and decisions. As St. Thomas so wisely counsels, "Even as false is found with true, so is evil mingled with good, on account of the great variety of these matters of action wherein good is often hindered by evil, and evil has the appearance of good. Wherefore, we need caution, so that we may have such a grasp of good as to avoid evil" (*ST*, II-II, Q. 49, art. 8). Again, prudence operates in that daily realm where we find few simple textbook answers. (If only I could search an index for the prudent course of action in my dilemma!)

St. Thomas, echoing Aristotle, notes that we cannot attain the same measure of certainty with differing subject matters. When prudence grabs the reins to drive our virtues toward practical goals in daily life, we can rarely be certain that we have chosen the best possible means to get there. But by exercising caution, we give time for all of the other essential parts of prudence to exercise their sway, thus giving us the best chance of hitting the virtuous targets at which we aim.

Unearthing Your Ten Talents

The Practical Wisdom of the Greeks

If the annexed parts of prudence — ευβουλια, συνεσιξ, and γνομε — appear to be all Greek to you, it is, of course, because they are. St. Thomas encountered *eubolia*, *synesis*, and *gnome* in the ethical writings of Aristotle. They address issues related to prudence, but do not call forth the virtue of prudence in full.

Eubolia comes from Greek words meaning "good counsel." The person with the virtue of *eubolia* seeks counsel from the wise when faced with complicated moral decisions. (Note, if you will, its relationship to docility, since it implies a willingness to learn from others). In discussing *eubolia* and *synesis*, St. Thomas nicely lays out prudence as a three-step process. In exercising prudence, we must:

- consider alternative courses of action (which we elicit through *eubolia*, or good counsel);

- judge the best alternative (this good judgment of ethical alternative is *synesis*), and finally;

- issue the self-command to act on that judgment, which is indeed the defining act of *prudence* itself.

So what about *gnome?* Well, it is not one of the steps of the process of prudence (neither has it to do with little bearded creatures). *Gnome* refers to the ability to cast wise practical judgments in extreme or unusual cases. (Perhaps King Solomon's effective suggestion to cleave in twain the baby of the disputing mothers is a biblical example of *gnome* in action.)

So, if prudence is the prize we seek, most prudent it would be to learn about and practice all these essential and related virtues that walk with it on the path of practical wisdom.

The Church Prudent

You've heard of the Church Militant and the Church Triumphant. Why not the Church Prudent as well? St. Thomas reports that when Church Fathers sought to discern special relationships between the seven virtues (cardinal and theological) and the seven sacraments, prudence was paired with the sacrament of Holy Orders. (Please see the appendix to spy all the correlations.) The Catholic Church puts those who are called by God to the religious life through a rigorous training and preparation of mind and spirit before they are ordained. Through docility, they will grow in the wisdom of Christ's Church, and through the guidance of the Holy Spirit, they will show their practical wisdom in their acts of reverence and service to God and to their flocks.

One member of a religious order long ago provided us with a lasting act of service by explaining the gift of the Holy Spirit that corresponds to prudence. That religious friar was St. Thomas Aquinas, and the gift is that of *counsel*. When we receive the gift of counsel, our actions are not only guided by our human reason, but are moved by the "Divine" and "Eternal Reason" of God. Please recall that "the gifts of the Holy Ghost are dispositions whereby the soul is rendered amenable to the motion of the Holy Ghost" (*ST*, II-II, Q. 52, art. 1).

So, although we must always exercise our human powers of reason in attempting to arrive at prudent decisions, we must also keep our souls open to the divine counsel wherein God speaks directly to our hearts. Exercising the *talent* of prudence, then, is not just all about us. In making major practical decisions that affect our lives and those of others, we must leave room for faith as well as reason, for prayer as well as syllogisms!

Of course, laymen, as well as religious, are called to develop the talent of prudence. Scripture tells us, after all, "if anyone loves righteousness, her labors are virtues; for she teaches self-control and prudence, justice and courage" (Wisd. 7:8). There are our talents of living. We'd be wise to accept the wisdom of Solomon, and to labor alongside with righteousness, in developing these virtues.[9]

[9] Oh, about that decision. While going through all the parts of prudence again and again for several days, with plenty of *eubolia* (good counsel from others), I found myself leaning strongly one way and then another and back again. The arguments were so closely matched, I felt this was more a job for *the gift of counsel*, and I tried to let go and allow myself to be receptive to God's counsel. I felt that I was moved — to stay. I'll try to shine whatever light I've been given and to unearth whatever talents I possess in the same position for now, and I do have faith that I was guided to the prudent decision this time.

PROFILES IN TALENT #9

Papal Prudence:
Pope John Paul II the Great (1920-2005)

Let's see how John Paul II personified the parts of prudence.

Memory: In spurring the demise of repressive communist regimes in Poland and elsewhere, he would remind massive crowds to remember their grand Christian heritage and national identities.

Understanding: He was a true master of applying universal principles to practical situations, such as in the way he used his profound understanding of Scripture to give us a *theology of the body* to guide our actions as sexual human beings.

Reason: Read the encyclical *Fides et Ratio* ("Faith and Reason") to see how he carried on St. Thomas's grand message of the role of reason in the lives of Christians.

Docility: He was willing to listen to and learn from all, from the most profound philosophers to the unschooled workers of third-world countries.

Shrewdness: The first pope to master mass media, he was able to think on his feet and rapidly respond with Christian wisdom in the most trying of situations.

Foresight: Think simply of what JPII's World Youth Days have done to revitalize the Church for this new millennium.

Circumspection: JPII was able to see issues from all angles, partly because he circumnavigated the globe, seeking firsthand knowledge through travel.

Caution: When advocating for human rights, he took care not to endanger those living under repressive regimes.

Part III

The Talents of Loving

"Those who have charity seek to love for the sake of loving, as though this were itself the good of charity, even as the act of any virtue is that virtue's good. Hence, it is more proper to charity to wish to love than to wish to be loved."

St. Thomas Aquinas

Chapter 8

Fostering Faith

"In order that a man arrive at the perfect vision of heavenly happiness, he must first of all believe God as a disciple believes the master who is teaching him."

St. Thomas Aquinas

"There are no real virtues unless faith is presupposed . . ."

St. Thomas Aquinas

The talents of loving transcend and transform the talents of learning and of living. They are built upon the natural intellectual and moral virtues, but these talents — faith, hope, and charity — go beyond what is natural. They perfect us not only as *biological* beings, but as *theological* beings, created in the image of God, for the purpose of enjoying eternal bliss in his company. The talents of loving are the theological, God-given virtues, infused in us through the graceful gift of God.

Faith is the foundation of all of the virtues. As we see in St. Thomas's second quotation on the title page of this chapter, there is no real virtue without it. This chapter, then, will proceed a little differently from the others. Before we consider the specifics of the uniquely precious talent of faith, I'd like us to begin by pondering another parable.

The Parable of a
Father's Precious Gift

Neither long ago, nor far away, a father gave a precious part of his own wealth to each of his newborn sons, knowing that each was destined someday to journey to foreign lands before they might return to him. (It was a generous and sizable sum — what the ancients might call a "talent.")

Each boy, for a time, treasured the fortune he had received, adding to it in small ways for years with the coins that came his way as gifts, or with the fruits of his own labors. Near the end of adolescence, each went on his separate journeys: the first son not straying far from home, but the second and third covering great distances, far from the sight, and almost the remembrance, of their father's land.

As full-grown men, they returned to their father and showed him what they had made of their precious gift. The first son, who had not strayed far, was pleased to show his father how his talent had grown, leaving him plenty to bestow a similar amount upon his own newborn son. The father beamed and promised this son even more.

The second son returned from his far-off journeys, having squandered all that he had added to the fortune; all he could show his father was the original sum. But he did come back with an attitude, chiding his father, "Why, I haven't even seen you for years, yet you expect to receive profit and interest from me, when you have been absent and idle." The father was not pleased, and he distributed this son's talent to his other two sons (and they proceeded to share it with others).

The third son had gone far away, out of his father's sight (although never his mind) for a long time. At one point, he, too, had nearly squandered his fortune away, but by the time he returned to his father, it had grown immensely, enough to share with his own new family, his friends, and his neighbors as well. The father was delighted and promised his son even more gifts, commensurate with his achievement.

What is the point of this modern parable? Of course, it is merely a variation of our thematic parable of the master and the servants (borrowing a bit from the parable of the prodigal son, and perhaps from Dostoevsky's *Brothers Karamazov*, as well). But here's the twist: the talent that each son receives in this parable represents one particular talent, the talent of faith.

Our Three Sons

Often, children born today into households with some mea-sure of faith will add to it, grow, and learn the ways of God. But when adolescence comes, they develop greater mental capacities to think and choose for themselves, and they become ever more exposed to influences outside of home and church. The modern culture they encounter is oftentimes hostile to the messages of the Christian faith, urging unchecked pleasures, fostering the idea of pure self-seeking and of "doing unto others," before they get the chance (as is considered wise in this culture) to do something hurtful unto you.

The journey refers most specifically to the adolescent's time spent in college, and it has become increasingly common today, even in various Christian, and even Catholic, colleges to receive messages quite contrary to the faith. The first son in this parable represents those who never seriously question or challenge their faith during young adulthood. Maybe they are not exposed to the counter-arguments, or they simply pay them little attention. They never lose their faith, although it might stagnate. (Some psychol-ogists might say that their identity has been "foreclosed," formed unthinkingly without seeking and confronting challenges; but if their faith was solidly formed and maturely developed, it will be too strong to be shaken by the views that would have challenged or squashed the faith of the unformed and the lukewarm.)

The second son represents today's all-too-common situation of the youth who is convinced by his professors or the popular media that *faith* is something childlike, something for the gullible, naive, unwashed masses, whereas *science* is for the mature, the hard-nosed, the sophisticated and enlightened, the intellectual elite. They've heard how Darwin, not the Church, has the bottom line on the nature of the human race. They've been taught that the

Church kept man in ignorance and darkness until the Renaissance brought back to us the liberating knowledge of the ancient pagans, and the Enlightenment signaled the triumph of reason over primitive superstition. (Of course, in more recent years, the existentialists, postmodernists, constructivists, and assorted avant-garde intellectuals of various stripes claim to have found that reason itself is also outdated, and since reason is, of course, the very basis of rational argument, who can argue with them?)

In This Corner — Faith, and in This Corner — Reason

So far, so good. Let's looks at this from a *dialectic* perspective. The concept of the dialectic goes way, way, back, even to Aristotle and Plato (and St. Thomas was its surest master). We can lay it out in terms of a *thesis* consisting of some basic belief, a contrary belief or *antithesis*, and a new belief that is based on a grasp of the fundamental points of both the thesis and the antithesis — namely, a *synthesis*. A dialectic is sometimes shown with the thesis and antithesis at the left- and right-hand corners of the base of a triangle, with the synthesis at its peak. Let's use the *thesis* in the context of our parable to refer to *the factual contents of the faith* of modern young men and women. Let's use the *antithesis* to stand for *the common modern arguments against Christian faith* that they encounter in the media and in the academy.

In our little parable, the first son has stayed with his thesis, relatively untouched by the arguments of the antithesis. In modern parlance, he might be called a "cradle Catholic." The second son has been swayed by the antithesis and lost his faith to the modern sentiments that oppose it. In ancient parlance, he might be called an "apostate." Today, he might call himself an atheist or an agnostic, if he bothers to consider the issue and deal with "labels" at all.

But what of the third son? The third son was enticed by the antithesis as well, convinced for a time that faith just doesn't hold water. (Fortunately, the water of his baptism had actually been held tight within his soul. Baptism, by the way, is the sacrament paired by the ancient Church Fathers with the virtue of faith.) But son number three also kept his mind and his heart open, and with time, experience, and God's grace, he came to see that the posturing professors and sundry secularists had overstated their case. Their criticisms of the Christian faith were aimed at a straw man, not at the flesh-and-blood God-man. They failed to see that although science can tell us many things about how things in nature work and can be manipulated, it can never tell us *why* there is a nature and whether we *should* manipulate it. The most crucial issues of *metaphysics* (the ultimate nature of the universe) and *ethics* (the realm of morality, of right and wrong) lie outside of science's ken.

In any event, there are many "third sons" out there today, and I consider myself fortunate to be one of them, after having spent a couple of decades in second-son status. I had been convinced not so much by modern scientists (I've always found their attempts to address metaphysical and ethical issues rather lame and unenlightened), but by modern philosophers. Through the likes of Bertrand Russell (who said, "Who made God?") and Ayn Rand (who considered man himself the supreme being), I came to see religion as something that just didn't make sense.

Fortunately for me, though, in my early forties I came across a man who reconciled faith and reason like no one before him. Pope Leo XIII wrote that this is the man who had the intellectual power to draw modern minds devoted to science and reason back to Christ and the Church. That man, of course, is St. Thomas Aquinas, and it was his great synthesis of faith and reason in the *Summa*

Theologica that brought *me* to third-son (what some might call "re-vert") status. Lo, if only more young adults dissuaded of their faith by modern science would discover the writings of the Universal Doctor!

St. Thomas showed how faith and reason need in no way op-pose one another. Indeed, the God in whom we have faith is the God who bestowed reason and will as the defining characteristics of the human being. He wants us to use our minds and to choose what to think and believe. And, like Lord Russell, St. Thomas was also famous for a childhood question about God — not "Who made God?" (which shows a lack of understanding of the differ-ence between a creature and a Creator) but "What is God?" Thankfully for us, we can read what his most powerful intellect and devout heart made of this question throughout his adulthood. Indeed, along with Pope Leo XIII, I argue that those who seek out the writings of St. Thomas and take the trouble to use their minds to learn about the faith (and let God work in their hearts) will stay in (or come back to) the Church.

So, if you'll forgive me the philosophical and personal digres-sion, let's go through a quick rundown of what the Universal Doc-tor tells us about the talent of faith itself.

What Is Faith?

St. Paul tells us that "faith is the assurance of things hoped for, the conviction of things not seen" (Heb. 11:1). Faith, then, implies a certainty (assurance) and belief (conviction) of the things of God that we are unable to see with our eyes, or detect with any of our senses, in our earthly state. What is it that we hope for? Eternal life. What is it that we cannot see? God himself. And what is the object of certain belief? The ultimate truth, which is God.

St. Thomas notes that the word *article* derives from the Latin word *articulus*, meaning "a small part or division." The English word *articulation* is another word for "joint," such as the elbow. The various articles of faith that appear in the great creeds, such as the Nicene Creed, which we recite during Mass, lay out the fine-tuned articulations that bind our religion together.

But there are fundamental mysteries from which the smaller articles of faith derive. These fundamentals of faith, St. Thomas explains, are the Holy Trinity and Christ's Incarnation. We cannot see the Holy Trinity with our eyes, nor can we see Christ's Incarnation.

Through the power of *reason* that God gave us, we can demonstrate that God exists (Rom. 1:19-20) and that he is fundamental truth and unity, but it is only through his revelation, which we accept on *faith*, that we come to know that his nature is *triune*, and that he *became man*. Through these fundamentals come the many related beliefs that make up our faith, and as St. Thomas notes, as time marches on throughout the centuries, the articles of faith may grow and increase, as man's understanding of divine revelation continues to flower. (Please see the two-thousand-year history of the Catholic Church for details.)

So, these are the fundamental objects of the Christian faith. But what is the *talent* of faith? How does faith operate *within us* to transform and perfect us in the image of God?

St. Thomas tells us that, whereas *hope* and *charity* (coming soon to chapters near you) reside primarily in the will, *faith* resides primarily in the *intellect*. Its object is truth, so it bears close relation to those intellectual virtues of science, understanding, and wisdom, as well as its theological partners of hope and charity. Let's consider six ways that our intellects may arrive at, or assent to, truths.

SIX APPROACHES TO TRUTH

Understanding: to grasp self-evident principles.
Science: to derive conclusions by reasoning.
Doubt: to incline to neither side of an issue.
Suspicion: to incline to one side on slight account.
Opinion: to incline to one side, but fear for the other.
Belief: to believe with certainty the unseen.

St. Thomas points out that beliefs derived from what we can perceive and reason about with certainty (the stuff of the intellectual virtues of *science* and *understanding*) require little effort on the part of the will. Our assent or agreement with truths that are before our very eyes, through the direct observation and reasoning of science (yes, the telescope does show little dots around Jupiter that we deduce are moons) or our assent with truths that stand as self-evident, ingrained in our very intellects through understanding (it is hard to convince oneself, for example, that one plus one does not make two), are direct intellectual processes. It is when grappling with truths that we can't completely grasp with our eyes or intellects alone that the *will* comes into play.

Let us look now at beliefs about God. Some may *doubt* God's existence. They may have no firm belief one way or another, thinking perhaps that they just don't know, or as with the agnostics, that we cannot know whether God exists. The doubters give no assent of their will one way or another. They neither believe nor disbelieve. In the words of St. Thomas, "Some of the acts of the intellect have unformed thought devoid of a firm assent" (*ST*, II-II, Q. 2, art. 1). This is the nature of doubt.

Others may *suspect* God's existence or non-existence, "but on account of some slight motive." There may be many questions in our lives for which we only suspect an answer, we "have a hunch," but rightly recognize that the issue does not warrant further consideration. Regarding matters of the Christian faith, however, there is nothing on this earth or beyond it more worthy of further consideration!

Another incomplete state of belief is seen in cases of *opinion*. Here one tends to believe one way or another, yet fears that perhaps he is wrong and the alternative is true. It will be hard for those who merely opine that God exists to live their lives in imitation of his Son.

True *belief*, though, is akin to the certainty that we obtain with science and understanding. Through the gift of God's grace, he who has faith and believes in God "cleaves with certainty to one side" — God's side. Thus, theologians and philosophers write of "leaps of faith" and "the will to believe," because faith is not a matter of logical deduction.

Faith does not, therefore, *oppose* reason, mind you. St. Thomas argued long ago that there can be only one truth, at which faith and reason are different means of arriving. Faith comes into play in the matters of things unseen, things that cannot be grasped directly through our senses — yet! Indeed, St. Thomas tells us that faith is a talent that will not persist in heaven, because in heaven *those things unseen will then be seen*. Those things we now *hope for in the future* will be *enjoyed in the eternal present*. We will not need to believe in God through faith, when the time comes that we can acquire direct knowledge of God through the Beatific Vision.

But that is later. For now, we need faith, in a big way. To have faith means that we trust in God and believe that what he has revealed, in Sacred Scripture and through his Church, is true.

Even though faith is a virtue that perfects our intellects and wills, it is not a natural virtue but a gift from God. He infuses it into our hearts, using both our intellects and our wills. St. Thomas tells us that faith requires two main things: first, that the subject-matter of faith is made known to us (requiring the intellect), and second, that we assent to the contents of faith (requiring the will). God plays a part in both processes, through direct revelation or by sending of prophets and evangelists that makes divine things known to us, and by preparing our wills to assent to these truths.

St. Thomas points out that revelation itself is not a sufficient cause. A person may experience the gospel message or even witness a miracle, but can still choose not to believe in God. Therefore, our actions that build the talent of faith are "meritorious" — pleasing to God "insofar as they proceed from the free will moved by the grace of God" (*ST*, II-II, Q. 2, art. 9). The ultimate merit for our faith, of course, is eternal salvation.

Bringing Your Talent of Faith to Life

"You believe that God is one; you do well. Even the demons believe — and shudder" (Jas. 2:13). St. James later tells us, "For as the body apart from the spirit is dead, so faith apart from works is dead" (2:26). St. Thomas tells us about both "lifeless faith" and "living faith." What is it that produces the works that make faith come alive? A hint: St. Paul called it the greatest of virtues (1 Cor. 13:13).

According to Thomas, "Each thing works through its form. Now, faith works through charity. Therefore, the love of charity is the form of faith" (*ST*, II-II, Q. 4, art. 3). It is Christian *charity*, then, that enlivens or "quickens the act of faith." Charity is that God-infused perfection of the will that seeks to share God's love with our neighbors. Charity itself will receive its rightful due in chapter 10. For now, let's remember that a true and living faith is *not* a matter of belief alone. The true Christian does not accept Jesus into his heart and then go on his merry way, without regard for the welfare of others or for the virtue of his own actions. The virtue of a living faith will serve as the foundation for all of the talents, leading us to develop them not merely for self-aggrandizement, but for helping our neighbor, doing honor to the generous Master for bestowing such wonderful talents upon us all.

PROFILES IN TALENT #10

Gratia Plenae, Theotokos: The Virgin Mary

If those titles seem "all Greek" to you, well, one is. Let's first examine the Latin title and then move on to the Greek. *Gratia plenae* is the Latin for "full of grace," and lest anyone think this is a mere "tradition of men," bear in mind that it was the angel Gabriel who addressed her in this way (Luke 1:27) before assuring her, "The Lord is with you." Mary was unusually blessed with the graces of God, including, of course, the theological virtue of faith. She completely personified "the assurance of things hoped for, the conviction of things not seen." Although her mind was first troubled by Gabriel's strange greeting, she believed what he foretold and willingly submitted herself to God's will in her famous *fiat: "Let it be to me according to your word" (Luke 1:36)*.

Being "full of grace," Mary possessed all of the talents in the greatest abundance. She is also referred to, for example, as the "Seat of Wisdom" (my copy of St. Thomas's *Summa Theologica* is dedicated to Mary under that title). Recall, too, that St. Thomas tells us that faith is "quickened," or made alive, through the virtue of loving charity. Working through the grace of God, it was Mary's loving charity that quickened, or made alive, in human form Charity himself. This is why she who is called "the mother of Jesus" and "the mother of the Lord" in the Gospels was declared at the Council of Ephesus in A.D. 431 to be *theotokos*, "the mother of God" (in the literal Greek, "God-bearer") for blessed was the fruit of her womb — and her faith.

Chapter 9

Harnessing Hope

"Insofar as we hope for anything as being possible to us by means of the divine assistance, our hope attains God himself, on whose help it leans. It is therefore evident that hope is a virtue, since it causes a human act to be good and to attain its due rule."

St. Thomas Aquinas

"The proper and principal object of hope is eternal happiness."

St. Thomas Aquinas

How easy it is to let the talent of hope lie buried in the earth, since it is precisely the things of the earth that can so easily keep it hidden! Distracted as we are, each day, and well-nigh all day, by the sights and sounds of the modern world, who has time to think about eternal life with God?

Enter the talent of hope. *Hope addresses our desire to be with God in eternity and to obtain his help in getting there.* Now, what we see around us is good, all right, but what is to come will be Good with a capital G — so good, in fact, that we really can't fathom it here on earth.

St. Thomas says that all of the theological virtues have God as their object. Faith, we saw, resides in the *intellect* and perfects our *knowledge* of the *truth* of God. Charity, as we will see in the next chapter, resides in the *will*, and expresses our *desire* and *love* for God (and, as a corollary, for our neighbors and ourselves). But what about hope?

Hope, like charity, resides in the will. And like the concupiscible and irascible appetites, hope relates to the goods that we love and desire. Hope, then, expresses our desire for eternal life with God, and as a talent of loving, it works to perfect our actions here on earth. As with faith, in heaven hope will not be needed, since we will not need to look to a future of blessedness when it has already arrived.

But now, here on earth, we're in desperate need of hope to perfect our wills and to please our Master. Let's begin to dig in, then, to see what St. Thomas has unearthed about this unearthly talent.

Hope, Connected with Faith and Charity

Hope builds upon faith and is brought alive by charity. We cannot hope for eternal bliss with God, and for his help in attaining it, unless we know of God and his promises through the eyes of faith. And as there can be a "lifeless faith" that knows of God but is not animated by charity, so, too, can there be a lifeless hope, which seeks its own eternal bliss without "the first love of God" that "pertains to charity, which adheres to God for his own sake" (*ST*, II-II, Q. 17, art. 8).

True, living hope, then, is informed by the mature understanding and heartfelt conviction of the talent of faith, and made alive by the love of God and of others, for their own sakes, that shines forth through the brilliance of the talent of charity. It is through this living hope imbued with charity that we anticipate not only our own salvation, but our neighbor's as well. The three talents of loving grow together best like three verdant vines, reaching intertwined toward the sun and through the Son.

No Mean Virtue?

St. Thomas addresses the argument that hope would seem to be more a moral virtue (a talent of living) than a theological virtue (a talent of loving), because moral virtues are matters of means between extremes, whereas theological virtues are not. Indeed, hope can be seen as a mean between the vices of *presumption* (a sin against the Holy Spirit wherein we presume our salvation is assured with no effort on our part) and *despair* (an opposing sin against the Holy Spirit in which we give up any hope of heaven, rejecting God's generosity and mercy).

But St. Thomas reminds us that the moral virtues relate primarily to things of man that are governed by reason, whereas the theological virtue "is concerned with the First Rule" — the things of God, governed by divine truth. Therefore, "hope has no mean or extremes, as regards its principal object, since it is impossible to trust too much in the divine assistance; yet it may have a mean and extremes, as regards those things a man trusts to obtain, insofar as he either presumes above his capability, or despairs of things of which he is capable" (*ST*, II-II, Q. 17, art. 6). We should be boundless, then, in our hope of the happiness that God has in store for us, yet wise and realistic when gauging our own capacities to determine how God might choose to assist us and act through us.

Hope also bears a relationship to the moral virtue of magnanimity (great-souledness) we addressed in connection to the moral virtue of fortitude. Hope, like magnanimity, regards an "arduous good," the bliss of eternal life being the supremely arduous and rewarding good that we can seek. Magnanimity, however, refers to obtaining goods within our own power, whereas hope desires that ultimate good which is possible only through divine assistance. Indeed, one manifestation of that divine assistance is God's very infusion of the talent of hope within our souls.

Fear: The Gift of Hope

"Fear of the Lord" is the gift of the Holy Spirit (Isa. 11:2) that corresponds to the virtue of hope. St. Thomas addresses a paradox here, since hope pertains to goods, and fear to evils. The fear of the Lord that is the gift of the Holy Spirit helps man hope for the good by helping him *avoid the evil that would deprive him of it.* God, of course, is the ultimate Good. Proper fear avoids the evil of the just punishment that God may administer if we turn from his ways, and of the privation we may suffer if we should come to a state of separation from him through our faults. There is more than one object of fear, and more than one way to fear. I'll let St. Thomas explain.

FOUR FORMS OF FEAR

Worldly fear: fear of loss of earthly goods or pleasure.
Servile fear: fear of punishment.
Initial fear: fear blending servile and filial fears.
Filial fear: fear of committing a fault.

Worldly fear is no gift of the Holy Spirit. This refers to our natural fears of losing the material goods or the sensual pleasures we desire. Neither is this kind of fear "the beginning of wisdom" (Ps. 111:10). Jesus himself advised us, "Do not fear those who kill the body but cannot kill the soul" (Matt. 10:28). For it is by abandoning our worldly fears that we can focus our attention on a proper fear of the Lord: a fear infused with love, a fear lest we become less than what is fitting for creatures made in God's image.

What St. Thomas, drawing on the writings of Sts. Paul and John (Rom. 8:15; 1 John 4:17-18) and of the Church Fathers, calls *servile* fear the lowest form of the Holy Spirit's gift of fear of the Lord. This is the fear of transgressing the laws of God out of a desire to avoid punishment. It is far from a perfect fear, in that it is not inspired by charity with the love of God for his own sake, but its object — the avoidance of God's displeasure and subsequent punishment — is good.

Initial fear derives from the Latin word *initium*, meaning "beginning." As the beginner starts to grow in a healthy fear of the Lord, *servile* fear and *filial* fear (a more perfect form of fear) might both be present. A man beginning to grow in charity, for example, might do the right thing both because he loves justice *and* because he fears to be punished for misdeeds. As his love for justice grows with time, his servile fear of punishment will fade away. As we read in 1 John 4:18, "Fear has to do with punishment, and he who fears is not perfected in love." Further, "perfect love casts out fear." As we grow in love, then, servile fear diminishes, and it is the increase of filial fear, the last and most perfect form, that leads to the perfect wisdom of charity. As we grow in our journey with God, and charity grows in our hearts, so, too, will the portion of filial fear come to predominate.

This more perfect form of fear of the Lord, conjoined with charity, is what St. Thomas calls *filial* or *chaste* fear. This is akin to the fear and deference that a son gives to his father or a wife to her husband out of affection and love. Here the object of the fear is the avoidance of committing a fault, of failing to live up to God's expectations for us. And here again we see St. Thomas's awareness of the potential of human spiritual growth and development. Seven hundred years after St. Thomas wrote the *Summa Theologica*, when modern psychologists began building theories of the development of moral reasoning, they started with the avoidance of punishment at the bottom rung of the moral ladder, leading to concepts of perfect justice and charity at its top. Indeed, St. Thomas calls us to strive continually to better ourselves, to unearth our talents and make ourselves complete, for the greater glory of him who made us. A healthy filial fear should inspire us all the more to develop our God-given talents for his honor and glory.

Poverty of Spirit: Fear's Beatitude

St. Augustine wrote that fear of the Lord befitted those blessed humble souls mentioned in the first beatitude, those who are "poor in spirit." Some have argued against this interpretation, noting that fear is the "*beginning* of wisdom," whereas the Beatitudes pertain, not to beginnings, but to *perfections* (or completions). St. Thomas tells us that "since a beatitude is an act of perfect virtue, all the Beatitudes belong to the perfection of the spiritual life" (*ST*, II-II, Q. 19, art. 12).

This does not exclude fear of the Lord from its direct correspondence to the beatitude of poverty of spirit. The filial fear that is wedded with charity is indeed a spiritual perfection. The person who through filial fear submits all things to God and seeks his greatness and richness in the things of God, embodies true poverty of spirit. Those with poverty of spirit need not renounce all earthly goods when these can serve as *means* of God's service, although those earthly goods will not be the *ends* in themselves — lest the insecurities bound with earthly fear replace the blessedness of filial fear perfected in those with true poverty of spirit.

Anointed with Hope

The early Church Fathers searched for spiritual meaning both in the Scriptures and in the products of man's own reason. So attuned to both faith and reason, they detected profound interconnections between the seven sacraments of Christ's Church and the seven virtues (the four classical cardinal virtues and the three Christian theological virtues). When they meditated upon the letter of St. James, the Holy Spirit led them to hope's sacrament. "Is there any among you sick? Let him call for the elders of the church, and let them pray over him and anoint him with oil in the name of the Lord" (Jas. 4:14).

In the sacrament of the Anointing of the Sick, the modern priest does pretty much just what St. James advised. He lays his hands on the sick individual, prays over him, and anoints him with oil (on the forehead and hands in the Latin rite of the Church), preferably oil that has been blessed by a bishop. This sacrament instills hope in the recipient: hope for physical healing, if it be God's will, and the ultimate hope in eternal bliss with God, if this illness should be his last.

Hope is also a most fitting grace and blessing for the sick and the dying, because its associated fruit of the Holy Spirit is patience — in this case, the capacity to endure the hardships that might ensue at life's end. Still, hope is also a precious talent that none of us should ever forget. We never know on which day we will be called to our Father's house, and hope can help us live every day on earth as if it were our last.

Bringing Hope to Life

"So faith, hope, and love abide, these three; but the greatest of these is love" (1 Cor. 13:13). The love that is charity is the greatest of all of the theological virtues. It is charity that transforms lifeless faith into living faith, hope for the sake of oneself into hope for the sake of God, the servile fear that avoids punishment into the filial fear that seeks to please God. When we unearth the talent of hope, we set our sights on eternal bliss with God and on the assistance he'll provide us in attaining it. So, next we turn to charity, that pinnacle of God-provided assistance, the last and the greatest of all the talents that make us most like him who made us.

PROFILES IN TALENT #11

Handing Hope to Modern Man:
Gilbert Keith Chesterton (1874-1936)

"Hope means hoping when everything seems hopeless," said G. K. Chesterton, who wrote during a time when many modern men and women were drunk on modern theoretical cocktails of Darwinian progress and socialistic, materialistic utopias. The past was passé; the future was the thing. Having thrown off the shackles of medieval superstitions, humanity was poised and ready for the superman, guided by reason (and perhaps with a bit of a genetic boost through the newfound science of eugenics).

Boundless progress and happiness stood around the corner when the rosy-fingered dawn of the twentieth century greeted young man Chesterton. Of course, while the twentieth century brought unparalleled technological advance, so, too, were tens of millions deprived of life, liberty, and the pursuit of happiness in modern godless regimes.

Chesterton brought real hope — for moral progress in this world and eternal happiness in the world to come. He said, though, that man needs to face the future as Perseus faced the Gorgon, not directly, but looking back at the mirror in hand, that mirror being lessons learned from the past. He saw man's greatest hope in that "everlasting man," Jesus Christ. "The Christian ideal has not been tried and found wanting," he said. "It has been found difficult, and left untried." Fortunately, Chesterton wrote prolifically on those lessons from the past that can guide us to a better future.

Chapter 10

Cherishing Charity

*"Charity is itself the fellowship of the
spiritual life, whereby we arrive at happiness;
hence, it is loved as the good which we desire
for all whom we love out of charity."*

St. Thomas Aquinas

*"Charity is essentially a virtue ordained to act,
so that an essential increase of charity implies
ability to produce an act of more fervent love."*

St. Thomas Aquinas

*"Charity is said to be the end of the other virtues,
because it directs all other virtues to its own end.
And since a mother is one who conceives within herself
by another, charity is called the mother of the other
virtues, because, by commanding them, it conceives the
acts of the other virtues, by the desire of the last end."*

St. Thomas Aquinas

This chapter's title on the talent of charity is meant to be taken quite literally. The first quotation from St. Thomas comes from his explanation of why we should love *charity itself, out of charity.* We should indeed cherish charity, the greatest of the talents we're given here on earth.

Something of such importance should raise a lot of questions. (It raised 143 questions in the articles of the *Summa Theologica!*) You might wonder, "Why is charity the greatest talent? What exactly is charity? Is it the same as love? Is it a state of mind? To whom should we direct it? How is it like friendship? Where does it come from? What are its effects? What works against charity? Can we build it in ourselves? How does it relate to our salvation? Will charity exist in heaven?" Some might even ask, "What's in it for me?" These are but a few of the legitimate questions we'll address.

The second quotation highlights the very active nature of charity. It is essentially (that is, at its very core) a virtue "ordained to act," says St. Thomas. So it's time for us to get into action right now, to examine the greatest talent God has given us, the talent that directs every single other talent to its proper end. It also happens to be the greatest talent we can give back to God, to our neighbors, and to ourselves — with interest.

Charity Is True Friendship

St. Thomas starts his examination of charity by explaining how it is a special kind of friendship, specifically, "the friendship of man for God" (*ST*, II-III, Q. 23, art. 1). How do we know this? Well, Scripture tells us so. Jesus said, "No longer do I call you servants . . . but I have called you friends" (John 15:15). Further, St. Paul, from whom we were given the most beautiful description of charity in the thirteenth chapter of his first letter to the Corinthians, also wrote in that same letter, "God is faithful, by whom you were called into fellowship of his Son, Jesus Christ our Lord" (1 Cor. 1:9).

But if we are to be the friends of God, we must ask ourselves what it really means to be a good friend. Just what is the nature of friendship? You've probably guessed that this question occurred to St. Thomas, too, and that he addressed it very thoroughly! Of course, you're quite right. Beginning on earth, with Aristotle's theories of the nature of human friendship, St. Thomas ascends all the way to heaven and our friendship with God, presenting us with three kinds of friendship:

- Friendship of utility;

- Friendship of pleasure;

- Friendship of virtue.

We all have friendships based to some extent on utility. We tend to befriend (and be befriended by) those who can be helpful to us, or whom we can aid in some way. Friendships built in school or in the workplace often start at this level. We gravitate toward those who might be able to give us a little help or advice, or perhaps to those to whom we can offer some expertise. This is all fine and good, as far as it goes, but utility is the lowest rung of the ladder of friendship. When taken to an extreme, it might not represent much of a friendship at all. Consider the "user" who values a friend only for what the "friend" can do for him. What happens if you are no longer of use to the user? No, true friendship, as an embodiment of the love of charity, is not entirely about one's own benefit.

The next step up the ladder is the friendship based on pleasure. It says not only, "I value what you can do for me," but, "Your presence is pleasant to me." This might build upon the first level of friendship. Perhaps your friend first helped you learn to play a certain sport, and now you enjoy pursuing it together with him, and even just talking about it. This tells your friend that you value not only what he had done or can do for you, but that you value something about his person.

At this level of friendship, you acknowledge that there are things in the other's personality or character, perhaps a sense of humor, hopefully an embodiment of some talent or virtue, that make it pleasant for you to be around him. But this level of friendship also has its limits. It still says that you value your friend for what he gives to you; in this case, not help but pleasure. What will happen to your friendship if he ceases to please you (or you cease to please him)?

The third and highest level of friendship is the friendship of virtue. This is the friendship that embodies true charity. The true friend has a love and concern for the welfare of his friend; the focus of this friendship is not on the good you can receive, but on the good that you can give to another. Aristotle notes that "very likely friendships of this kind are rare" (*Nichomachean Ethics*, Bk. 8).

His main reason for saying this? "Virtuous men are scarce." You see, in order to have a loving friendship based on one's own virtue and the love of the virtue in another, the friends themselves must be virtuous. Apparently, even in fourth-century Athens in the Golden Age of Philosophy, such friends were hard to find. These, of course, were the days before the coming of Christ and the establishment of his Church. With the wisdom we can obtain from

Scripture and Tradition, and with the sacraments and graces of the Church at our disposal, there is no need today for virtuous souls — or friendships of virtue — to be scarce. Remember, then, as we build our talents, we also build our capacity for true friendship; friendship with our neighbor and with God.

Aristotle gives another reason for the scarcity of virtuous friendships: true friendships require time and familiarity. He cites an old proverb that two people don't know each other "until they've eaten a peck of salt together." Friendships of virtue take time to develop — time for friends to become more familiar, learn each other's virtues, face life challenges together. Because they are based on virtue, on deeply ingrained habits of character, rather than on things such as usefulness or pleasure, friendships like these are also built to last.

These principles apply as well to the friendship we build with God. It takes time. We must immerse ourselves in his Word, pray and converse with him daily. We must strive to make him the center of our thoughts and our being, day after day. And no friend will be truer than this One.

Yes, true virtuous friendship is one aim of charity. Jesus told us that the end of all the laws is summed up in the charity we express toward God, our neighbors, and ourselves. Interestingly, it is in his section addressing how sinners do not properly love *themselves* (*ST*, II-II, Q. 25, art. 7) that St. Thomas, expanding upon Aristotle, shares five elements of true friendship, five things that true friends desire and do for their friends:

- You desire your friend to be, to exist.

- You desire good things for your friend.

- You do good deeds for your friend.

- You take pleasure in your friend's company.

- You are of one mind with him, rejoicing and sorrowing in almost the same things.

By true friendship, I refer to the virtuous friendship discussed above, which Aristotle also called "perfect" or "complete" friendship. First off, we obviously desire that our friends exist and live. The death of a friend is a cause for true sorrow. It might feel as if we have lost a part of our self. Do we stop to thank God that it is through his bounty that our friends exist and have become known to us? Do we demonstrate our appreciation for our true friends' existence, both to them and to God?

Next, we desire true good for our friend. Unlike the partial, seeming, or incidental friendships of utility and pleasure, in true friendship we don't want the goods just for ourselves, but for our friend as well. Thirdly, just as actions speak louder than words, so, too, do actions speak louder than thoughts or desires. Scripture tells us, "Let us not love in word or speech but in deed and truth" (1 John 3:18). St. Thomas elaborates, "Now, the love of neighbor requires that not only should we be our neighbor's well-wishers, but also his well-doers" (*ST*, II-II, Q. 32, art. 5). In other terminology, St. Thomas notes that the second element is a matter of *goodwill*, while the third is a matter of *benevolence*. True friends, imbued with charity, *feel* goodwill and *act it out* in benevolent deeds.

What about taking pleasure in the friend's company? Isn't pleasure the basis of that second form of partial, incomplete friendship we addressed before? Yes, it is. But true friendship brings deeper pleasures still. In true friendship comes the pleasure we derive from a friend's virtue: from his character, his charity, his embodiment of the talents God gave him. He need not amuse us with his wit to give us pleasure. The very self he has crafted himself to be, and his willingness to share it with us, gives us a deeper and more lasting pleasure.

There's another important aspect of this element that cannot be forgotten. Note that friends take pleasure *in one another's company*. Although "absence may make the heart grow fonder" for a while, prolonged absence from friends might set the stage for another maxim — namely, "out of sight, out of mind." Aristotle notes that friendships are often lost through a lack of interaction over time. Our modern world makes it so much easier to wander apart from our friends, but it also makes it easier to keep in touch. Those simple things — the thoughtful call, the brief email greeting — that reconnect us with our friends can provide some form of the "company" that is necessary to keep pleasure alive and to show our friend that he is still in our hearts.

Someone once said (actually, I imagine a lot of people have said something along these lines) that at the end of life, most of us will probably regret not so much some horrible thing we've done as the multitude of opportunities for the little goods we could have done, but didn't. Along these lines, in expressing the talent of charity, let's try to be ever more mindful of those little acts we can direct to our friends to show them that their very being still brings pleasure to our hearts, even though they may be far away.

And let's never forget the ultimate object of our charity and friendship. How deep, then, should be the pleasure we derive from our friendship with God? How much time do we spend immersed in the pleasure of the friendship extended to us by the embodiment and perfection of all human and divine virtue — Jesus Christ?

The last feature of true friendship is a oneness of spirit, of attitude and outlook. Aristotle described true friendship as "one soul in two breasts." Truly virtuous friends, immersed in the exercise of charity, will certainly have their own unique preferences for a variety of minor things — foods, sports, clothing, and so on — but when it comes to the truly important matters in life, issues of faith and morals and living out the Christian calling, virtuous friends will find great affinity. The same kinds of things and events will bring them joy (an effect of charity that we'll soon discuss.) So, too, will similar happenings bring them sorrow.

It is here that St. Thomas, with psychological profundity, notes that the sinner most completely fails in love *of himself*. Virtuous friends are of the same mind because they're in agreement in their love of the truly good things that come from God. Their focus is on the goods of the higher, "inward man": spiritual things, virtuous deeds, things that glorify man's rational nature with an intellect and will made in God's image. So, too, when the man of virtue looks into his own heart, he finds good thoughts, good memories of the past, and good hopes for the future. He finds pleasure within his own heart, since his will is undivided.

In contrast, the sinner who has turned his back on God and failed to cultivate his talents has focused on his lower sensual and bodily nature. Even when he looks inside his own heart, he finds discord and clashing of will. He cannot find pleasure in his own heart. His memories of past deeds bring forth "gnawings" of conscience.

Please take a minute to look at and memorize those five elements of true friendship. We should reflect each day on how we can develop our talent for true friendship steeped in charity, and how we can direct it to God, our neighbors, and ourselves.

There's a famous saying (and song title): "Love is a many-splendored thing." So it is. Let's move along now to take a look at some more of its splendors.

The Mother of All Talents

St. Paul has told us that charity is the greatest of the theological virtues (1 Cor. 13:13). St. Thomas chimes in that charity is the "mother" of all the virtues, since "every virtue depends on it in a way" (*ST*, II-II, Q. 23, art. 4). All the *moral* virtues depend on prudence to determine the right means to put them into action. Prudence, remember, is that practical wisdom that seeks virtuous means to attain virtuous ends. But how do we determine which *ends* are virtuous? Truly virtuous ends are those that derive from the rule of charity. When Jesus summed up the law and the commandments to tell us to love God with all our hearts and our neighbors as ourselves, he commanded us to live the life of charity. God is the most virtuous, highest, and last of all ends. Charity resides in the will, and the will desires, seeks, and loves the good. The love of charity seeks the highest good, attainment of union with God.

The love of charity is an active love. It is expressed in works; not only in goodwill, but in benevolent behaviors; not only in kind thoughts, but in good deeds of all stripes. It reaches out to all. St. Thomas compares the love of charity to the heat of a powerful furnace. When our hearts burn with the fires of charity, their far-reaching flames will serve to warm strangers and even our enemies. But as those closest to the furnace receive the most heat, true charity should begin at home, and be directed in greatest intensity to the Spirit who dwells within our hearts, and to those who are near to us — our families, friends, school- or workmates, neighbors, and fellow parishioners.

When charity prevails, it brings great inward effects, such as the joy that comes when desires are fulfilled. This joy will see its complete fruition in heaven. Charity also brings with it peace, both the peace that reflects love and concord between different people, and the peace that reflects harmony within one's own soul, as the intellect, will, and appetites rest in tranquility in their united focus on God.

The Degrees of Charity

St. Thomas's brief discussion of the "degrees of charity" (*ST,* II-II, Q. 24. art. 9) is brimming over with theological insight, practical usefulness, and perhaps even some illumination on a mysterious event in the life of the Angelic Doctor himself. Although charity, as a theological virtue, is infused into our hearts by God, it can increase or decrease through our actions. St. Thomas tells us with moving eloquence how each act of charity increases within us the disposition or tendency for more charitable acts, "and this readiness increasing, breaks out into an act of more fervent love, and strives to advance in charity, and then his charity increases actually" (*ST,* II-II, Q. 24, art. 6).

Aristotle says that we become builders by building and harpists by playing the harp. So, too, Thomas tells us we become fervent lovers by loving fervently! And indeed, as promised in the heading, he tells us how this plays out in three degrees of increasing perfection:

- Resistance of sin

- Development of virtue

- Pursuit of oneness with God

Charity, we are told, increases in a way analogous to growth in human development, from the incapacities of infancy to the manifold powers of full maturity. The first degree of charity, akin to our infancy in the spirit, focuses primarily upon the avoidance of sin.

Unearthing Your Ten Talents

When we first turn our hearts to God in earnest, we have a battle on our hands and must curb and contain many vices, many habitual earthly tendencies to seek out our animal and sensual goods at the expense of higher intellectual and spiritual goods. We are all imperfect sinners by nature, and we must always remain on guard, but the first degree of charity remains the lowest. This degree of charity seeks primarily to avoid the evil, while the next degree focuses more clearly on doing the good.

Indeed, some commentators have noted that part of the power of St. Thomas's writings was that, unlike many theologians and teachers of his day and of previous days, who focused heavily upon sin and depravity, St. Thomas focused much more on the positive message of how we can grow spiritually. While never ignoring our sinful nature (his insightful catalogue of various sins and vices is peerless), St. Thomas also urges us to heed more completely Christ's call to "be perfect as your heavenly Father is perfect" (Matt. 5:48).

At the second degree of the development of charity, the pursuit of virtue takes center stage. Here's how St. Thomas describes it: "In second place, man's chief pursuit is to aim at progress in good, and this is the pursuit of the proficient, whose chief aim is to strengthen their charity by adding to it" (*ST*, II-II, Q. 24, art. 9). Unearthing and developing one's talents is clearly, then, a second-degree pursuit!

Although pursuing virtue is a noble and efficacious means of squelching sin, those with charity of the second degree must still continue to fight the good fight against their sinful appetites, if and until their attainment of true virtues comes to still this internal discord completely. Thomas quite graphically compares this task to those who built the walls of Jerusalem while fighting off their enemies, who "with one hand labored on the work and with the other held his weapon" (Neh. 4:17).

And what of the third and highest degree of charity? "Man's third pursuit is to aim chiefly at union with and enjoyment of God: this belongs to the perfect *who desire to be dissolved and to be with Christ*" (*ST*, II-II, Q. 24, art. 9). Thomas tells us that the rare and saintly souls who attain this third degree can still grow in charity, but their main concern is in union with God.

For most of St. Thomas's adult life, he wrote and taught, sharing with his peers and with all who have come after him how we can grow in virtue, especially in the crowning virtue of charity. Yet, the story is told that near the end of his life, he had a vision after which he declared that all of his work had been "as straw." After that he wrote little more until his death at age forty-nine. The summary of the *Summa Theologica* he'd been working on, and even the *Summa Theologica* itself, massive as it is, were left incomplete.

The significance of this episode has given rise to conflicting opinions, from those who saw it as St. Thomas's repudiation of his own work, to those who interpreted it as a medical issue, most likely a stroke. In any event, consider that event along with St. Thomas's descriptions of the degrees of charity and with one more extraordinary event recorded about his life. It is said that St. Thomas beheld a vision of Christ himself. When Christ asked Thomas what he wanted, his answer was, "Only you, Lord." Is it possible, then, that near the end of his life, St. Thomas had broached that third degree of charity, restless for anything but union with God? Could the "straw" that was his theological works have been the kindling that fueled the fires of charity that brought him to that exultant state?

Charity and Christ's Church

"Greater love has no man than this, that a man lay down his life for his friends" (John 15:13). When the early theologians paired the virtues with the sacraments to highlight their common-alities, it just made sense that charity, the highest of the virtues, would be paired with the Eucharist, the greatest of the sacraments. In every Mass we celebrate anew that greatest of all acts of love.

Throughout the last two thousand years, the Catholic Church has striven to spread Christ's loving charity throughout the world. One of its teachings, one that bears directly on the virtue of char-ity, is its ages-old endorsement of the spiritual and corporal "works of mercy," whereby "we come to the aid of our neighbor in his spiritual and bodily necessities" (CCC, par. 2447). Things such as advising and counseling, as well as feeding and clothing our neigh-bors, St. Thomas, tells us, are actually "acts of charity through the medium of mercy," since "the love of our neighbor requires that not only should we be our neighbor's well-wishers, but also his well-doers" (ST, II-II, Q. 32, art. 1, 5).

The Principal Act of Charity Is Love

Charity *works*. It gets good jobs done. It gives form and life to all of the virtues. Infused by God, it reigns supreme in loving good-ness over the talents of learning and the talents of living. If we have all the other talents, but lack charity, we are but clanging gongs and cymbals; we gain nothing (1 Cor. 13:1-3). It is the most precious of all the talents, a talent that *must* not remain hidden under the earth. The light of charity within our souls should never be hidden under a wicker basket, but should shine forth among men. As St. Thomas tells us, the principle act of charity is to love, not only in good thoughts, but in good deeds. Let's ask ourselves, the minute this book is set aside: how can we, right now, do some small act of charity for someone around us? Then let's do it!

PROFILES IN TALENT #12

No Greater Love Than This:
St. Maximilian Kolbe (1894-1941)

At the end of July 1941, a prisoner escaped from the Auschwitz concentration camp in Poland. The camp commandant randomly selected ten men from the same cell-block to be starved to death for this transgression. One of the chosen men began to wail aloud for the fate of his poor wife and children.

Standing by was a prisoner, Franciscan Father Maximilian Kolbe, who had a special devotion to Mary. He had started a "Militia of Mary Immaculate," edited a paper called the *Knight of the Immaculata*, and actually founded cities of Mary Immaculate in Poland, Japan, and India. A holder of doctorates in philosophy and theology, he had expounded a simple mathematical formula for making oneself a saint, namely $v = V$, where v = your will and V = God's will. (Charity, you'll recall, resides in the will, *voluntas* in Latin.) In his last letter he wrote, "If virtue consists in the love of God and of all that which springs from love, evil will be all that which is opposed to love."

Father Kolbe boldly asked to take the place of the condemned man with the family, and his offer was accepted. About two weeks later, on August 14, the vigil of the feast of the Assumption of Mary, when Father Kolbe and three others had failed to die from starvation and the Nazis had need for the cell, he was given a lethal injection of carbolic acid. St. Maximilian had taken a vow of poverty, but he lived, breathed, and died fabulously rich in the talent of charity.

Part IV

The History and Practice of the Talents

*"Let him who has understanding look that he
not hold his peace; let him who has affluence
not be dead to mercy; let him who has the art of
guiding life communicate its use with his neighbor;
and him who has the faculty of eloquence intercede
with the rich for the poor. For the very least endowment
will be reckoned as a talent entrusted for use."*

St. Gregory the Great

Chapter 11

Top Theologians Tackle
the Tale of the Talents

*"This lesson from the Gospel warns us to consider
whether those who seem to have received more in this
world than others shall not be more severely judged
by the Author of the world; the greater the gifts, the
greater the reckoning for them. Therefore, everyone
should be humble concerning his talents in proportion
as he sees himself tied up with a greater responsibility."*

St. Gregory the Great

*"To him who has faith, and a right will in
the Lord, even if he come to aught short in deed
as being man, shall be given by the merciful Judge;
but he who has not faith, shall lose even the other
virtues which he seems to have naturally."*

St. Jerome

We have interpreted the talents as ten great virtues perfected within our souls through the bounteous grace of God. Having seen the importance St. Thomas attached to the virtues, I can't help but think he might have approved of our project. And I believe that he would be the first to remind us that in order to truly exercise our intellectual talents of understanding, science, and wisdom, we must take counsel from the greatest minds and most devout souls who came before us. So what did those great ancient Fathers have to say about our parable? What inheritance can we reap from them? As you might expect, we can turn to St. Thomas — whom Pope Leo XIII praised for having "the utmost reverence for the doctors of antiquity" — to find that out.

It's not his longest work by a long shot (the translation I use is a mere 990 pages), but don't be fooled by its relative brevity — St. Thomas's *Commentary on the Gospel of St. Matthew*, also called the *Catena Aurea* ("Golden Chain"), contains commentary from an impressive array of the most talented theologians from the Church's early centuries. In this work, he devotes about ten word-dense pages to our parable of the talents, with dozens of comments from the likes of St. Jerome, St. Gregory the Great, St. John Chrysostom, St. Hilary, and Origen. Let's see what they can teach us.

A Golden Chain of Talents

In the parables that follow, I'd like to produce some of the feeling (and, I hope, some of the insight) of St. Thomas's treatment of the various Fathers' comments on the elements of this parable. I'll be paraphrasing, paring, and pruning things down in this presentation, but I pray that perhaps you'll feel prompted to peruse the commentary itself to ponder these pearls from our pastoral patriarchs. All right, alliteration aside, let's get down to the brass tacks. (I mean golden chains. And, oh yes, my own commentary on the commentary will be found *in italics*.)

Chrysostom observes that the parable is intended to warn those who will not assist their neighbors with their money, words, or deeds; this is what it means to hide one's talents away. Origen points out that the Master is, of course, our Redeemer, Jesus Christ. Gregory notes that his "journey far away" is Christ's ascent into heaven. An ancient theological gloss notes that the Master's far journey indicates that the servants were left to their own free will and choice of action during his absence.

Jerome notes that the varying number of talents relates to the diversity of gifts we have been given. Origen adds that the differing number of talents relates to our diverse degrees of capacity. He also makes the point we made earlier: that even one talent was by no means a small amount.

As to the meaning of the talents, Origen indicates that the man who received five talents is able to see a divine significance in the Scriptures, while he who received only two has carnal or worldly knowledge. Gregory compares the five talents to the five senses, the two talents to understanding and action, and the one talent to understanding only. Jerome also relates the five talents to the five senses, and he indicates that by using his senses, the man doubled his knowledge of heavenly things "from the creature understanding the Creator, from earthly unearthly, from temporal the eternal."

As Aristotle and St. Thomas elaborate so well, knowledge, understanding, and wisdom all depend first upon the information fed to the intellect by the senses. Please recall previous sections in chapter 1 on the operations of the sensitive and intellectual soul, and the section on "the birth of an idea" in particular. Even much of our knowledge of God derives from what we see reflected in his creation.

St. Gregory chimes in that even those who cannot "pierce to things inward and mystical" can profit from the senses that bring us into direct contact with the "things without," especially when they can teach others not to be inordinately absorbed with those externals — with the lusts of the flesh, ambition for earthly success, and inordinate delight in things seen. He notes, too, that those who by their understanding and action preach to others gain "a twofold profit." They also double their talents when they teach what they have learned to members of both sexes.

Origen notes that "healthy conversation" with others exercises the senses and aids in their increase to higher levels of knowledge and to a desire to teach others.

Recall St. Thomas's observation from chapter 2 that "a characteristic of one possessing science is the ability to teach." Also note that teaching others about the faith is among the spiritual works of mercy.

On the importance of what we can learn from others in the full development of our talents, Origen notes, "No one can easily have increase of any virtues that are not his own, and without he teaches others what he himself knows, and no more."

Does this call to mind the virtue of docility, and of counsel, both as a part of prudence, and as a gift of the Holy Spirit?

St. Hilary relates the talents to the Judaic Law and to the gospel of Jesus Christ: those who accept Christ double their talents, while hiding a talent in the ground "is to hide the glory of the new preaching through offense at the Passion of his body." Origen points out that the servants do not come to the Master, but the Master comes to them, after a long delay, to judge them. He indicates that the Master has allowed time for his servants to become fit and capable, "to bring about the salvation of souls." He then comments on the relatively long lifespans of the Apostles and St. Paul.

Even in men such as those, true talents are not built in a day, but are a project for a lifetime.

Chrysostom, too, comments on the delay, noting that we are to learn of "his long-suffering" alluding to Christ's death and Resurrection. Jerome refers to the long delay as the time between Christ's Ascension and his Second Coming.

In any event, we can see how this delay calls on us to develop the perseverance of the virtue of fortitude and to enjoy the Holy Spirit's fruit of longanimity.

At this point in the commentary, we find Gregory's comment that I used as the first quotation to grace the beginning of this chapter.

Here we see that the more gifts and talents we receive from God, in whatever particular form they may take, the greater is our responsibility to build them, to exercise them for good, and to remain humble, as we recall God's role in giving us the powers to build them.

Next in the golden chain of commentary, our great commentators address the Master's reactions to the servants who doubled their talents.

Here we see the ultimate purpose or "end" of the development and sharing of one's talents. Alas, dear reader, I must ask you to wait for the ultimate chapter of this book before I share their wisdom — and reveal the "eleventh talent."

The Fathers also address the situation of that servant who chose to bury his talent under the ground. Jerome points out that the servants who started with five talents and with two were looked upon with "equal favor" by the Master. Origen notes that all God requires is that whatever talents a person receives from God should be used by that person for all they're worth for the glory of God.

Truly, then, the Master would have taken the same delight in receiving two talents from the least "talented" of his servants as in receiving ten from his most talented.

But what of the man who buried his talent in the earth? Gregory notes that in failing to trade with his talent, he offered to his Master not talents but "words of excuse." In offering "excuses excusing sin," Jerome notes that he added the sins of slothfulness and idleness to the sin of pride.

This servant told his Master through his actions that he had better things to do than to make the effort to use the talents he gave him.

Origen notes that the first servant came to the master with "boldness." *This bespeaks of a proper magnanimity or greatness of soul. The last servant's demeanor, however, smacks of presumptuousness, that vice of excess that thinks it knows better — better than even the Master. Recall, if you will, from chapter 4 on the parts of fortitude, what St. Thomas had to say about the actions of this last servant. Whereas Jerome describes how the servant confronts the Master upon his return with presumptuous behavior, that sham of excess that mimics magnanimity, Thomas notes that his initial act of burying the talent embodies pusillanimity, the "fainthearted" smallness of soul that fears to employ one's talents. Our servant, then, timidly shirks his own responsibility in making use of his talent, and then brazenly seeks to blame the Master, who had given him the talent in the first place!*

Jerome notes that the last servant would have done much better to have acknowledged his fault and sought forgiveness from the Master. *(We know from other parables that this is the Master who wrote the book on forgiveness and mercy.)* Origen also compares the last servant to those who believe in Christ, but conceal their faith so that others may not know they are Christians.

This sounds to me like the faith without works "which is dead" (Jas. 2:26.) Recall that the greatest Christian talent is that of charity, that charity brings life to faith, and that charity's principle act is to love. If people cannot see that we are Christians by our love, to what extent are we living as Christians?

Gregory compares this servant to people within the Church who set out to live a better life, "yet are not afraid to continue in carnal indolence," failing to seek true holiness and remaining content "in their own iniquities."

Jesus asked us to take up our cross and follow him. The unfaithful servants are those who are afraid to test its weight upon their backs, unmindful of the fact that at the end of the day, all who labor and are heavily burdened will be given rest.

What about the servant's reproach of his Master, who "sows where he does not reap and gathers where he does not winnow"? Origen notes that the righteous man sows in the spirit and reaps eternal life and that the Lord "counts as bestowed upon himself, all that is sown among the poor." Jerome indicates that we can also interpret this reaping where he did not sow as God's bringing into his Kingdom the "Gentiles" and the "Philosophers." Hilary, too, notes that the "fruits of righteousness" would be reaped where the Law was not sown, indicating that the Lord will also reap souls among the Gentiles not born of the seed of Abraham.

Jerome remarks that the Master called the servant "wicked" because he "caviled against," or reproached, his Lord, and "slothful" because of his inaction. *(Recall again that excess of presumptuousness and that deficiency of pusillanimity.)* He was told that he should have invested with the bankers to return the talents "with interest." Jerome tells us that the talents are actually the preaching of the gospel, and the "heavenly word" and the bankers are actually the Doctors of the Church. The Apostles did this when they ordained priests and bishops to spread the good word.

Gregory writes as well that as the teachers of the good news are expected to teach, so, too, are the hearers of the gospel, so that "from what they have heard they should strive to understand what they have not heard."

Note that the call to exercise the intellectual talent of understanding is a call to every one of us.

As to the Master's actions toward the unfaithful servant, we know that he took his talent from him and gave it to the man with ten, "for to everyone who has, more will be given, and he will have abundance; but from him who has not, even what he has will be taken away." Gregory writes that this shows the true importance of charity, that he who has the talent of charity receives the other gifts also, but he who does not have charity loses all the other gifts that he "seemed to have."

Surely you recall the words of St. Paul and St. Thomas on the fundamental value of the talent of charity, as underpinning and providing the impetus and setting the end for the working of every other talent — every virtue, every gift, every power we share in common as humans, and every unique ability, talent, skill, or expertise that any one of us might obtain.

Chrysostom, Jerome, and Hilary all chime in on similar themes. The talents are to be used and shared with others. They are based on faith in Christ and expressed through loving charity.

Wrapping Up the Golden Chain

And what of the ultimate fate of those who bury their talents and of those who return them to the Master "with interest?" We'll examine this in the concluding chapter.

Unearthing Your Ten Talents

We have seen but a glimpse of the fruits that the parable of the master and the servants has produced in the minds of some of the most thoughtful Fathers of the Church. Would you agree that they saw the talents as something akin to the virtues we have been addressing? Surely we vary a great deal in our individual skills and abilities, but the kinds of talents involved in building virtue within our souls, and sharing our virtues with others, are there, in potentiality, for us all. And we need not start with the greatest of natural gifts to produce the most benefit for our neighbors.

Consider the talents of learning. Raw intellectual capacity varies, of course, from person to person. But all of us have intellects, and we can all make the best use of them by seeking to become as wise as we can in those spiritual things of the greatest importance. And sometimes we can learn the most about the talents of living and loving that matter most from those who are least gifted in the talents of learning. As many a person who has worked with the mentally challenged can attest, we can learn much about life and love from those genuinely special individuals, gifted as they are in their own unique manner.

As for the most general lessons of the learned theological Doctors, recall how the Fathers stress the importance of *action* and of *teaching*. We are all here to teach and to learn from each other, to share our talents, and to grow in them through conversation, interaction, and joint projects of good works. This is a far cry from hoarding our talents for ourselves, or burying them in the earth.

In our next and penultimate chapter, I'd like to suggest some very practical methods we can use to unearth and develop the talents within ourselves, to share them with our neighbors, and to return them to our glorious Master, with the kind of interest that will find him well pleased.

PROFILES IN TALENT #13

A Most Multitalented Father (and Papa):
St. Gregory the Great (540-604)

Read the works of St. Thomas Aquinas, and time and again you'll see the name and the insights of St. Gregory the Great cropping up. (Indeed, he provides the first quotation for this chapter of this book.) Check out a Catholic encyclopedia, though, and you will see that St. Gregory wasn't really a philosopher, or an innovative theologian. So why was he so influential, and "Great" to boot?

Recall how St. Gregory advised us to exercise humility in whatever talents we possess. Gregory had a profound influence on medieval theologians, partly because of his respect for earlier Church Fathers and for the Scriptures. (No wonder St. Thomas admired him.) He compiled and synthesized the writings of earlier great thinkers and rendered them accessible to his peers and successors. His own greatest talents, however, were as a leader and as a bishop. He even wrote a book for bishops, stressing their role as "physicians of souls." The bishopric that most fully exercised Gregory's talents was that of the diocese of Rome.

St. Gregory, the first monk to be Pope, strengthened the monastic systems within the Church, extended the reach of Christ's Universal Church throughout the world, and solidified the jurisdiction of the Roman Apostolic See, and of the papacy, over all the churches of the world.

Chapter 12

Ten Tools for Turning Up the Talents

"The object of our inquiry is not to know
what virtue is but how to become good."

Aristotle

"Virtue is that which makes its possessor
good and his work good likewise."

St. Thomas Aquinas

"For all that is required is that whatever a man has
from God, he should use it all to the glory of God."

Origen

Here's one more issue for your consideration (and, I hope, inspiration) before we get down to the practical techniques to build the talents within our souls. All sorts of philosophical and psychological theories have hit upon the same pair of themes that sum up man's strivings on the earthly plane. Aristotle defined man as the "rational animal," but also described him as the "political animal." Modern psychological researchers have examined the fundamental "need for achievement" and the basic human "need for affiliation" as well. Psychiatrist Alfred Adler emphasized that we have powerful inherent "strivings for superiority," but that to achieve mental health and well-being, these strivings must be guided by "social interest." Some refer to these affiliative or social needs as "horizontal strivings," because they represent our reaching out to others. The achievement or perfection-based needs are referred to as "vertical strivings," as in "climbing the ladder of success."

When Adler talked about this basic need for superiority, he did not mean superiority over others, but rather, self-improvement. We start in the world as helpless infants, and as we grow, we become aware of our incapacities. We develop a burning desire to grow, to become more competent and confident in our powers. (Witness the young boy's fascination with the competent and powerful heroes of comic books.) This is a good and healthful thing — when it grows alongside what Adler called "social interest" (our best translation from his German *gemeinschaftsgefuhl*). Social interest refers to a feeling of social rootedness or connectedness, and caring for others. The key to mental health is to fulfill our needs for self-improvement, "superiority," and achievement in ways that manifest "social interest."

Divine Interest

Jesus has called on us to fulfill both of these basic elements of our humanity. Are we not to "be perfect" as our heavenly Father is perfect? Is not the highest of our goals, the greatest of the commands he has given us, to love God with all our hearts and our neighbors as ourselves?

The development of these talents, then, will bring out the very best in our humanity. We shall strive to achieve self-improvement, to become "great-souled," but only as directed by the charity that gives life to all the virtues and guides them, not only by a "social interest," but by a truly "divine interest" as well. We'll climb the ladder of spiritual success, not in order to get a rung ahead of others, but so that we may extend a hand to help others ascend with us, toward the last rung that leads to heaven.

Okay, then. We've *looked* at all ten talents, *analyzed* their meanings, *reflected* on the synthesis of their closely knit interrelationships with virtues, gifts, Beatitudes, sacraments, and each other, *considered* their relationship to psychological theories on man's deepest needs, and *pondered* their significance for this life and the life to come. Now, what are we going to *do* with them?

"Alas," you might say, "if only I had *time* to build these wonderful talents, what great and glorious treasures would I amass, great boons to myself, to humanity, and to the generous Master himself." Well, the Master truly is generous, and although each of us has his own apportioned earthly lifespan (and none of us knows its expiration in advance), the Master has been completely just and generous in granting us all the same twenty-four hours in every day. Ultimately, it is up to us to decide what we are going to do with them.

The virtues underlying the talents are essentially *good habits*, deeply ingrained patterns of behavior that make the most of our powers — habits "which make its possessor good, and his work good likewise." We build these habits by *learning* about the virtues, by *choosing* virtuous courses of action, and by *repeating* the virtuous acts day after day after day until they become as "second nature."

Let's look next, then, at ten practical suggestions for unearthing our talents and molding them into habits that will make their presence known every day of our lives. Like the talents themselves, these suggestions each tap into different, although related, aspects of our uniquely human capacities. No doubt you're already following some of them, but the idea here is to do them systematically, with the purpose of making your talents grow. I've labeled them as follows: read, memorize, act, attend, question, seek, simplify, exercise, pray, and love. Hence, to get started, all we'll need to do is to practice the first suggestion itself.

Read

Something tells me you're doing this one right now! Continued reading about the talents is a great way to increase your understanding of them, or just to keep them on your mind. I've culled bits and pieces of interest on the virtues, gifts, fruits, and Beatitudes that make up the talents, mostly from the second part of the second part of the great *Summa Theologica*, which remains the most complete source of information on these talents. St. Thomas also wrote a *Commentary on Aristotle's Nichomachean Ethics* that treats in great depth the virtues at the heart of the first seven talents. (This is also one of my favorite books outside of Scripture. It's fascinating to read one of the two greatest human intellects in history, digesting and explaining the work of the other. Indeed, it's two super-geniuses for the price of one!) I also suggest that you seek out St. Thomas's *Commentary on the Gospel of St. Matthew* to benefit more completely from the Church Fathers' interpretations of the parable of the talents. And don't forget Scripture, of course. Matthew 25:14-30 is the ideal starting point for your own meditations on the talents.

Memorize

Let's not forget that memory is the first and arguably the most fundamental part of the talent of prudence. When you come across concepts or quotations that stir your enthusiasm for the development of the talents, consider learning them "by heart" by committing them to memory. Starting very simply, how about the talents themselves? Have you memorized all ten? (You'll find a simple mnemonic for the talents of learning and loving in chapter 3 of *Memorize the Faith!*)

Next, were there any quotations in this book, from Scripture, from old Aristotle, from the Angelic Doctor, or from any other of the philosophers and theologians, that really struck a spiritual chord with you? Direct word-for-word memorization of quotations is best done the old-fashioned way: reading them out loud and repeating them time and again. Once memorized, further repetition, day after day, will help you remember to always seek to build and share your talents. Let's see if you can remember this one (courtesy of Origen): *For all that is required is that whatever a man has from God, he should use it all to the glory of God.*

Act

We know that our talents are of no use if they lie buried under the ground. In order to unearth them and build them, we must use them again and again and again. As Aristotle told us long ago in his *Nichomachean Ethics* (Bk. 1), "We become builders by building and harpists by playing the harp." Similarly, it is by doing just acts that we become just, by doing temperate acts that we become temperate, by doing brave acts that we become brave.

Note that prudence, that greatest of the talents of living, and charity, the greatest of the theological virtues (and of all of the talents), share in common their fulfillment in virtuous *acts*. Actions speak louder than words because actions get the job done. To fully develop our talents, then, we must be alert to the ways in which we can put them into action, each and every day. So please allow me to make a couple of simple suggestions, derived from the psychological and self-help literature I absorbed in the days of my youth.

• Do some small good deed *each and every day* that you would really rather just as soon *not* do. The deed may seem of little consequence. It could be the same thing every day, such as getting up five minutes early to read the day's scriptural readings, or something different each day — maybe offering to get up off the couch and go get something for your spouse, or make dinner that night. Be creative in these simple, habitual acts for strengthening your will.

• I believe it was the entrepreneur and writer W. Clement Stone who employed the slogan "Do it now!" as a self-admonition. When you realize you need to do some deed, be it completing some yard work, calling your mother, or simply getting up out of bed in the morning, and you have an urge to put if off and procrastinate, you will say to yourself, like Mr. Stone, "Do it now!" and immediately, like the good folks at Nike, "Just do it!" Got that? Train yourself so that whenever you say to yourself, "Do it now!" you *do it now.* But use this power of reason and will wisely. Always be sure to follow the statement with the action, and it will become habitual and effective.

Attend

Building talents means building virtues. Building virtues means building good habits. Building good habits means replacing bad habits. A habit is, of course, something that has become almost automatic in our lives — habitual. We hardly even have to think about it. We just do it. So, to replace bad habits, vices that can keep our talents submerged under the earth, we must become *aware* of our own thoughts and actions. We must strive to pay *attention* to what we are doing.

In my book *Fit for Eternal Life*, I wrote a bit about this in regard to replacing gluttony with temperance. We need to train ourselves to become aware of how much and how often we are eating. The same applies to the eradication of all vices and the building up of all talents. We need to pay attention to our own daily routines and behaviors.

"Look at that clock! How long have I been sitting here surfing the Internet or watching the boob tube? Aren't there better things I could be doing? Couldn't my Bible use a little dusting (or reading)? Didn't Aunt Martha ask me to come over and help her move something into her attic? Have I given any more thought to becoming involved in that group at church? How long have I been writing? Wasn't I supposed to pick up my son at school? Wait — my cell phone is ringing. Yep, it's my son, and he's waiting." (That last one, I'll admit, just happened to me moments ago.)

The bottom line is that we need to be aware of what we are doing, so that those automatic patterns of laziness or self-coddling won't deflect us from unearthing the talent buried right under our complacent, oblivious, and sleepy-headed noses.

Question

Along with attending, we also need to scrutinize ourselves. An ages-old technique favored by ancient Stoics and Christians alike was the examination of one's conscience right before bedtime. (Recall from chapter 3 how St. Thomas himself endorsed pondering spiritual matters before sleep.) We need to question ourselves at each day's end, asking to what extent we have striven each day to develop and share our talents.

And during the day, when we're wide awake, the various parts of the talents themselves can provide fodder for some profitable questions. To condense in brief what I wrote in *Memorize the Faith!* on the parts of the virtue of prudence, when I'm faced with a practical moral dilemma, I find it useful to ask myself to what extent I have applied each of those eight integral parts of prudence. Other important questions to ask ourselves could be drawn from the nature of virtuous friendships. As we prepare to encounter a friend, or build a new friendship, we can ask ourselves what actions we will take to show our friend that we cherish him not only as an object that meets our needs, but as a subject whose happiness (both on earth and in eternity) we desire.

Seek

To what extent are we really striving to develop our talents? One of the best ways I know to do this is to seek out models of virtue. This ties in to the first suggestion on reading. Plutarch, remember, wrote his lives of famous Greeks and Romans to inspire readers to emulate the virtues of those great men. In the Catholic Church, of course, we are blessed with a vast Communion of

Unearthing Your Ten Talents

Saints displaying a myriad of different talents, interests, and vocations. These can serve as great models of excellence, if only we seek them out — by reading through the stories of their lives, and by praying to them for their intercession. Which great saints will you seek to learn about, pray to, and imitate in their sharing of their talents?

Simplify

If we are to strive to develop our talents, we need to be truly focused on the essentials. If it's virtue that we seek, we cannot be constantly distracted by all of the diversions of the world. St. Thomas, you'll remember, contrasted the vice of *curiosity* with the virtue of *studiousness*. The curious are drawn here and there by all sorts of passing interests and events, whereas the studious focus on what is truly important. We must train our attention on the highest things, and let lesser things take care of themselves. To this end we must develop the discipline to turn off sources of media and enjoy regular periods of silence and repose.

The ancient Stoic philosophers valued virtue over all else. We do well to borrow one of their key ideas, which is to concern ourselves only with those things under our own control (essentially, our own thoughts, emotions, and behaviors), leaving the actions of others, and other events beyond our control, in the hands of God. When we focus simply on developing our virtue, we will be far less likely to stray from the virtuous path when others direct less-than-virtuous behaviors our way.

Exercise

We know that we are mind/body composites, and as Christians we believe that we will be resurrected on the last day — not just our soul but our body, too. While we're here on earth, the body needs tending, and this can be done through simple time-efficient strength-training and cardiovascular exercise. You'll find my full contribution to this field in *Fit for Eternal Life*, but our simple message here is to remember that our bodies are the temples of the Holy Spirit and that we are to strive to make them perfect. As St. Thomas has explained so well in his description of the nature of the human soul, the intellect, although immaterial, feeds on the data supplied to it by our bodies via our sense organs and our brains. By tending properly to our physical temples, we will be in the best shape to fill those temples with the treasures of the talents.

Pray

To develop our talents, we need to be in regular communication with the Master from whom all our talents flow. He crafted the human natures that make the talents of learning and living possible, and he instills in us, through his grace, the crowning theological virtues of faith, hope, charity, and the seven special gifts of the Holy Spirit. In the *Summa Theologica*, St. Thomas addresses prayer in the greatest depth under the discussion of the virtue of religion as it relates to the virtue of justice. It is eminently worthy of reading firsthand. At the end of this book, I have tried my hand at a prayer to acquire the talents, modeled after St. Thomas's prayer *Pro Obtinendis Virtutibus*, "To Acquire the Virtues."

Love

We've seen that charity is the greatest of the talents, and we've been told that its principal act is to love. This, then, we must surely strive to do above all. Love whom? God, and our neighbors as ourselves, of course. We are constantly provided with opportunities to exercise one of the simplest and easiest ways that love can be expressed and built, and it's "merely" through acts of kindness.

Unearthing Your Ten Talents

Kindness is a very important and delightful virtue in its own right. In the opening pages of *The Hidden Power of Kindness*, Father Lawrence Lovasik emphasizes that true kindness is not only passive and receptive, but is active and assertive. Kindness not only entails helping others when they ask, but trying to see things from others' perspective, being alert to ways that we might offer our services before they're asked for. After all, Jesus advised us to *do* unto others as we would have them do unto us, not just *respond* to them that way.

PROFILES IN TALENT #14

Virtue in Practice: Epictetus (c. 50-120 A.D.)

Slave poor as Irus, halting as I trod,
I, Epictetus, was a friend of God.

Anonymous Epitaph

One of the reasons our Catholic Church is so well suited to help us develop our talents is its respect for truth, whatever may be the source. Although they did not know Christ, there is much we can learn in living lives of virtue from the ancient Greek and Roman Stoics. Epictetus, a poor, freed slave with a lame leg (halting did he tread), was among the most humble and profound of all of them.

For the Stoics, our highest calling is to follow God by pursuing virtue. We do this by making a clear distinction between things outside of our control (including *everyone else's* behavior) and things within our control (*our own* attitudes, judgments, feelings, and behaviors.) *By training ourselves to become undisturbed by things we cannot control, we free ourselves to pursue the virtuous ends within our control (such as developing our talents.)* One way Epictetus recommends to develop your talents is to focus on your roles. Are you a father, mother, brother, employee, employer, parishioner, citizen? Then what are you doing to bring your talents to bear on being the very best father or mother or sister or brother or employee or employer or parishioner or citizen you can be?

Conclusion

The Best Is Yet to Come:
The Eleventh Talent

*"What greater thing can be given to a faithful servant
than to be with his Lord, and to see his Lord's joy?"*
St. Jerome

"By this word joy *He expresses complete blessedness."*
St. John Chrysostom

*"This will be our perfect joy, than which
none is greater, to have fruition in that
Divine Trinity in whose image we were made."*
St. Augustine

*"Final and perfect happiness can consist in
nothing else than the vision of the Divine Essence."*
St. Thomas Aquinas

So what is the eleventh talent? Particularly attentive and mathematically minded readers might suspect it is *art*. Why *art*, of all things? Well, look at the table of natural virtues in chapter 4. Aristotle described two intellectual virtues of the practical intellect: prudence and art. By *art* he doesn't necessarily mean the virtue of painting pictures, but the general capacity for making things. Art is not the eleventh talent of which I speak, however, for two main reasons. First, our conception of a "talent" refers to capacities we build within our souls, rather than material things. Secondly, the eleventh talent is not a natural virtue, but a supernatural gift. The "eleventh talent" is, in fact, the supreme supernatural gift: the Beatific Vision of God in heaven. Let's listen to our wise Church Fathers on this one.

Origen notes that the parable says that after a time the servants came to the Master, meaning that at the end of their lives they came before God. The Fathers agree that the servants are rewarded with the complete joy and blessedness that come from the vision and company of the Lord. St. Gregory adds that the faithful servants will be "numbered in the company of the angels" and that their joy will be complete.

Unearthing our ten talents will bring many spiritual rewards to us here on earth, and our neighbors will benefit from them as much as we will. The ultimate purpose of increasing our talents lies in the next life, however. Here on earth, we see "as in a mirror, dimly." We cannot fathom how great this reward will be.

Unearthing Your Ten Talents

I believe it was C. S. Lewis who compared the relation of heavenly joys to earthly joys to the relation between sexual pleasures and the pleasures of chocolate. The child whose highest delight is in eating chocolates is unable and unready to comprehend the higher, comparatively ecstatic delights of a loving, marital intimacy. So, too, are we who are immersed in earthly delights, unable to fathom what lies ahead in heaven.

Does the site of a majestic mountain range or the stars in the sky fill you with a sense of awe? Does the site of a beautiful face set your heart aflutter? Does a young child's smile put a smile on your face? Does it feel good when you accomplish some good deed, or when someone shares with you an unexpected kindness? Just think then: who is the ultimate source of every worldly delight? Who is the author of this world and the stars, and the creator of every beautiful face and every innocent child? God is the source of all good. We can't really begin to imagine the good that awaits us in his kingdom.

The keys to the kingdom lie within the talents God has given us, infused by his Holy Spirit to inspire us to live in the imitation of Christ. In that eternal kingdom, enjoying forever the Beatific Vision of the Holy Trinity, all of the human powers that underlie the talents will achieve their complete fulfillment. Our intellects, appetites, and wills, our bodies and our souls, will achieve their final end: ultimate truth and ultimate goodness.

The Beatitudes represent our complete joy in union with God in heaven. The talents are means of showing God that we seek to cooperate with him in making ourselves his worthy servants, taking good care of the little he sets us over on earth, so that he may set us over ever so much in his eternal kingdom.

PROFILES IN TALENT #15

Alpha and *Omega*: Jesus Christ

Jesus is the beginning and the end of all the talents. He also exhibits them to the highest degree:

• *Understanding:* Jesus is the foundation of all truth; in fact, he is "the way, and the truth, and the life" (John 14:6).

• *Science:* Jesus took on human form to obtain knowledge as we do: through the senses, guided by the intellect.

• *Wisdom:* There is no truer wisdom, no loftier knowledge, than the knowledge of Christ and the peace that flows from it.

• *Fortitude:* Need I mention the way of the Cross as the means to our salvation?

• *Temperance:* Jesus loved the world. He did not lust after it for his own gain.

• *Justice:* Jesus actually gives us all far more than our due.

• *Prudence:* Jesus chose the best means to his ends, painful as they were.

• *Faith:* Jesus literally *embodies* the absolute fundamentals of faith: the Trinity and the Incarnation.

• *Hope:* Jesus' Incarnation, Crucifixion, and Resurrection are the wellsprings of our hope. He has promised that we will share in his everlasting kingdom.

• *Charity:* "Greater love has no man than this, that a man may lay down his life for his friends" (John 15:13).

A Prayer to Acquire the Talents

O generous Master,
    beginning and end
    of all that is true and good,
Enlighten our minds
    with the talents perfecting the intellectual soul
    you gave us in your image.
Grant unto us
    knowledge of the wonders of your creation,
    understanding of the principles that lead us to truths,
    and wisdom to know, understand, and be glad in your
        ultimate truth.
Plant in our hearts
    the talents perfecting our appetites and desires,
    and the will that is also in your image.
Grant unto us
    fortitude to endure the hard things we must
        bear to win things truly good,
    temperance to reign in desires for false or
        excessive goods,
    justice to give to you and our neighbors
        all that is rightly due,
    and prudence to find the best means to pursue holy ends.

Unearthing Your Ten Talents

Infuse into our souls
    faith in things unseen,
    hope in the eternal kingdom to come,
    and charity to make every talent shine with love.
Grant that these talents may grow with interest,
    bearing their kindred virtues of godly character.
Grant unto us
    humility, to see how little we are without
        your gifts of grace,
    and to appreciate the talents you have
        given to our neighbors.
Give to us
    magnanimity, such greatness of soul, that
        despite our own weakness
    we may aim at great things, confident in you
        who strengthen us.
Help us
    seek honor,
    not through the accolades of our neighbors,
    but through the performance of worthy deeds.
Grant to us
    that our eyes may focus on the noble
        and the beautiful,
    and that our hands will never be busy
        burying the talents you have given us.
Help us share with others
    magnificence, not only in outlays of money,
        but in acts of caring,
    kindness, so that by attentiveness to
        the needs of our neighbors
    our talents will grow fastest by giving them away.

A Prayer to Acquire the Talents

Grant to us, too,
 heartfelt gratitude
 for all you so freely give.
Grant also that we may return to you
 more talents when you call at the journey's end
 than you gave us at its start,
 so that we who have been faithful with a little
 may be found worthy to be set over much
 and to bring you joy.
O bounteous and glorious Master,
 we know not the hour that you may call,
 but we pray that it finds us sharing
  talents with our neighbors,
 loving them, as we would have them love us,
 and as you love us all.

Amen

Appendix

A Table of Ten Talents

THE TEN TALENTS:
VIRTUES PERFECTED BY GOD'S GRACES

The Ten Talents (virtues)	The Seven Gifts of the Holy Spirit	The Eight Beatitudes	The Twelve Fruits of the Holy Spirit	The Seven Sacraments
Understanding	Understanding	Purity of heart	Faithfulness	
Science	Knowledge	Mourning	Faithfulness	
Wisdom	Wisdom	Peacemaking	Joy; peace	
Temperance	Fear	Poverty of spirit; purity of heart; mourning	Modesty; self-control; chastity	Matrimony
Fortitude	Fortitude	Meekness; bearing persecution	Patience; gentleness	Confirmation
Justice	Piety	Hunger for righteousness; mercifulness; peacemaking	Kindness	Reconciliation
Prudence	Counsel	Mourning	Goodness	Holy Orders
Faith	Understanding; knowledge	Purity of heart; mourning	Faithfulness	Baptism
Hope	Fear	Poverty of spirit	Patience	Anointing of the Sick
Charity	Wisdom	Peacemaking	Charity; joy peace	The Eucharist

When St. Thomas addresses the specific verse of Matthew 25:15, wherein we are told that the Master dispensed the talents to each servant "according to his proper *virtue*" (*ability* in the Douay and RSV versions), he notes "in this passage, *virtue* denotes not the natural ability alone, but the natural ability together with the endeavor to obtain grace" (*ST,* Suppl., Q. 93, art. 3). Note, then, from the very start of this parable, how the talents have a twofold nature, embodying both our God-given natural powers and our willingness to try to make the most of them through the grace of God. So the fully developed, full-blown talents are the fruition of our own continuing efforts toward virtue, enhanced and made complete or perfect through the supernatural grace of God.

The table at the left illustrates some of the interconnections and interrelationships gleaned from the golden wisdom of the Angelic Doctor. We were told in Sirach (3:29) that it's wise to ponder a parable. Perhaps these interconnections will warrant a little pondering as well, pondering that will inspire us to a little practicing and perfecting.

About the Author

Kevin Vost

Kevin Vost (b. 1961) works by day as a Public Service Administrator for the State of Illinois, overseeing a group of dedicated disability adjudicators. He has also served as a college psychology professor, weightlifting instructor, fitness writer, Research Review Committee Member for American Mensa, lector for St. Agnes Catholic Church, and fast-food fries and drink man (a few decades back). Dr. Vost, a self-styled Aristotelian/Stoic/Thomist, lives in Springfield, Illinois, with his wife, two sons, and two dogs. He welcomes your questions and comments at www.drvost.com.

An Invitation

Reader, the book that you hold in your hands was published by Sophia Institute Press.

Sophia Institute seeks to restore man's knowledge of eternal truth, including man's knowledge of his own nature, his relation to other persons, and his relation to God.

Our press fulfills this mission by offering translations, reprints, and new publications. We offer scholarly as well as popular publications; there are works of fiction along with books that draw from all the arts and sciences of our civilization. These books afford readers a rich source of the enduring wisdom of mankind.

Sophia Institute Press is the publishing arm of the Thomas More College of Liberal Arts and Holy Spirit College. Both colleges are dedicated to providing university-level education in the Western tradition under the guiding light of Catholic teaching.

If you know a young person who might be interested in the ideas found in this book, share it. If you know a young person seeking a college that takes seriously the adventure of learning and the quest for truth, bring our institutions to his attention.

www.SophiaInstitute.com
www.ThomasMoreCollege.edu
www.HolySpiritCollege.org

SOPHIA INSTITUTE PRESS

THE PUBLISHING DIVISION OF

 THOMAS MORE COLLEGE *of* LIBERAL ARTS    HOLY SPIRIT COLLEGE